Missouri Hauntings

Lee Prosser

Schiffer Publishing Ltd
4880 Lower Valley Road, Atglen, Pennsylvania 19310

Other Schiffer Books on Related Subjects:

Ghosts of St. Louis: The Lemp Mansion and Other Eerie Tales, 978-0-7643-2688-2, $12.95

Greetings from St. Louis, 978-0-7643-2824-4, $24.95

Copyright © 2009 by Lee Prosser

Library of Congress Control Number: 2008934391

All rights reserved. No part of this work may be reproduced or used in any form or by any means—graphic, electronic, or mechanical, including photocopying or information storage and retrieval systems—without written permission from the publisher.

The scanning, uploading and distribution of this book or any part thereof via the Internet or via any other means without the permission of the publisher is illegal and punishable by law. Please purchase only authorized editions and do not participate in or encourage the electronic piracy of copyrighted materials.

"Schiffer," "Schiffer Publishing Ltd. & Design," and the "Design of pen and ink well" are registered trademarks of Schiffer Publishing Ltd.

Designed by Stephanie Daugherty.

Type set in AmerType Md BT/ NewBskvll BT

ISBN: 978-0-7643-3119-0

Printed in China

Disclaimer
Many of the locations and settings in this book are open to the public. Others are on private property, condemned for safety reasons, and the owners would not appreciate uninvited guests. I urge you not to trespass on private property or anywhere else without permission. Please have respect for the current owners and their ghosts.

Schiffer Books are available at special discounts for bulk purchases for sales promotions or premiums. Special editions, including personalized covers, corporate imprints, and excerpts can be created in large quantities for special needs. For more information contact the publisher:

Published by Schiffer Publishing Ltd.
4880 Lower Valley Road
Atglen, PA 19310
Phone: (610) 593-1777
Fax: (610) 593-2002
E-mail: Info@schifferbooks.com

For the largest selection of fine reference books on this and related subjects, please visit our web site at: **www.schifferbooks.com**.

We are always looking for people to write books on new and related subjects. If you have an idea for a book please contact us at the above address.

This book may be purchased from the publisher. Include $5.00 for shipping. Please try your bookstore first. You may write for a free catalog.

In Europe, Schiffer books are distributed by
Bushwood Books
6 Marksbury Ave.
Kew Gardens
Surrey TW9 4JF England
Phone: 44 (0) 20 8392-8585
Fax: 44 (0) 20 8392-9876
E-mail: info@bushwoodbooks.co.uk
Website: **www.bushwoodbooks.co.uk**

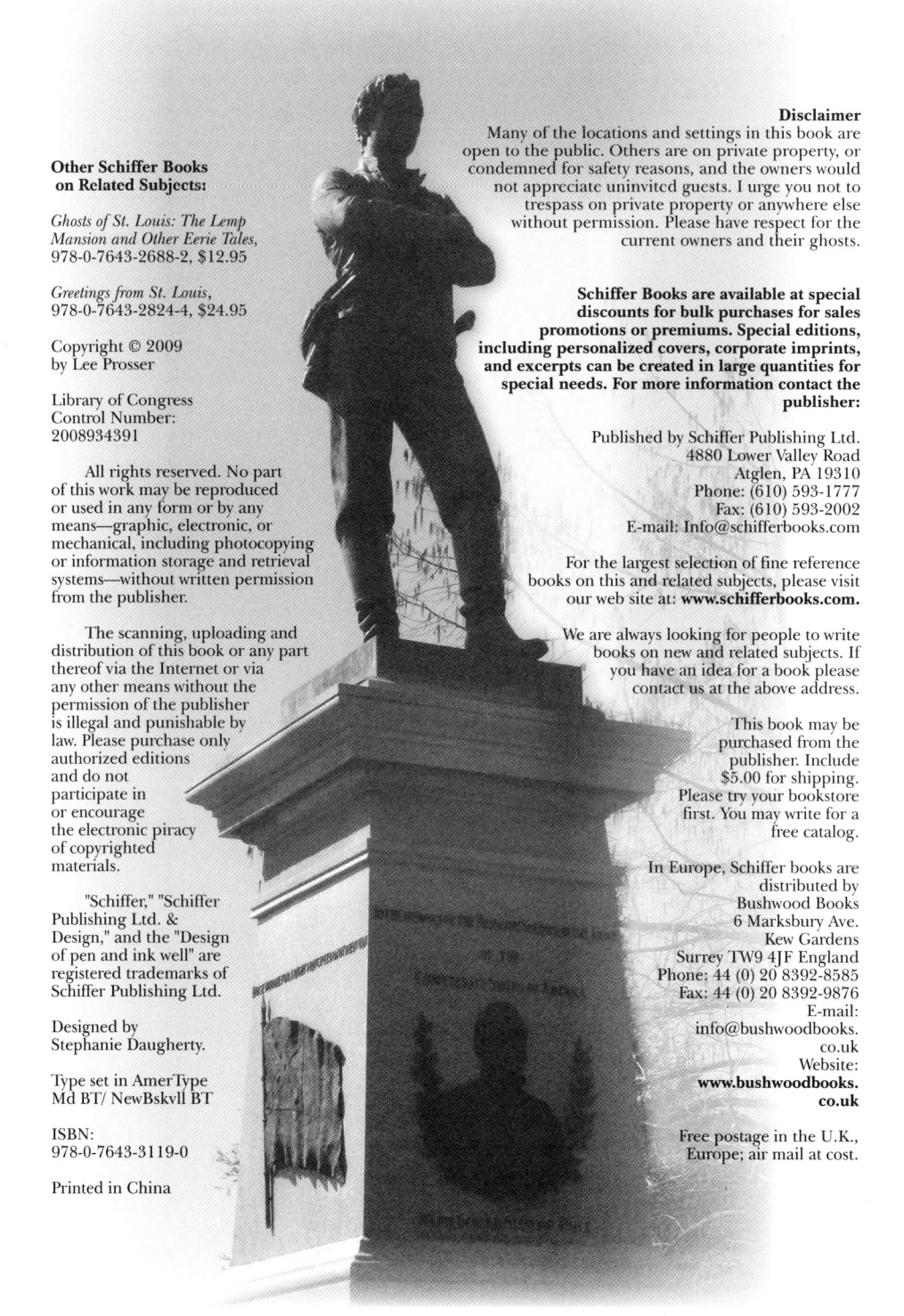

Free postage in the U.K., Europe; air mail at cost.

Acknowledgements

This book is dedicated to those I love, especially first and foremost, my wife Debra and my family. Thank you, Debra, for all the positive encouragement. I think of you with love every time I hear Cole Porter's song, "Night and Day," because you are the One. And to the following friends for various personal reasons and in appreciation for past kindnesses: Jeff Belanger; Gerina Dunwich; Don Bachardy; Swami Chetanananda; John Gilbert; Bonni Hamilton. Also, I thank my editors at Schiffer Publishing, Dinah Roseberry and Jennifer Marie Savage; Ray Bradbury, Swami Girijananda, Swami Nishpapanda, Devadatta Kali, Lon Milo DuQuette, and Alice V. Spencer.

I also wish to dedicate this book in memory of my late uncle, Willard David Firestone, who was my first guide and mentor to all things occult, supernatural, religious, spiritual, and paranormal. A pianist-composer, Willard David Firestone was an adept of many traditions. He taught me early on to keep my findings and occult education mainly to myself because of the general public's fearful ignorance of such things. In 2008, despite the important strides made in metaphysical research, the general public is still fearful, yet has now become infinitely more curious about all things supernatural and paranormal. Uncle Willard also taught me: "Death is only another door opening to a different reality. The soul is immortal, and if you believe the soul is immortal, then the possibility of reincarnation becomes a reality."

With that in mind, it becomes even more pertinent what Swami Chetanananda told me many years ago: "Be good, and do good. Do good, and be good." Swami Chetanananda is an internationally known writer, speaker, minister, and spiritual teacher at the Vedanta Society of Saint Louis, Missouri.

I share the following with those interested in communicating with ghosts: 1 Corinthians, 12:10. Also, there are many faiths in this world, and as Sri Ramakrishna observed, "As many faiths, so many paths."

I also dedicate my book to the many individuals I visited or came into contact with during my investigation of the hauntings in Missouri. Many thanks. Bright blessings to all of you!

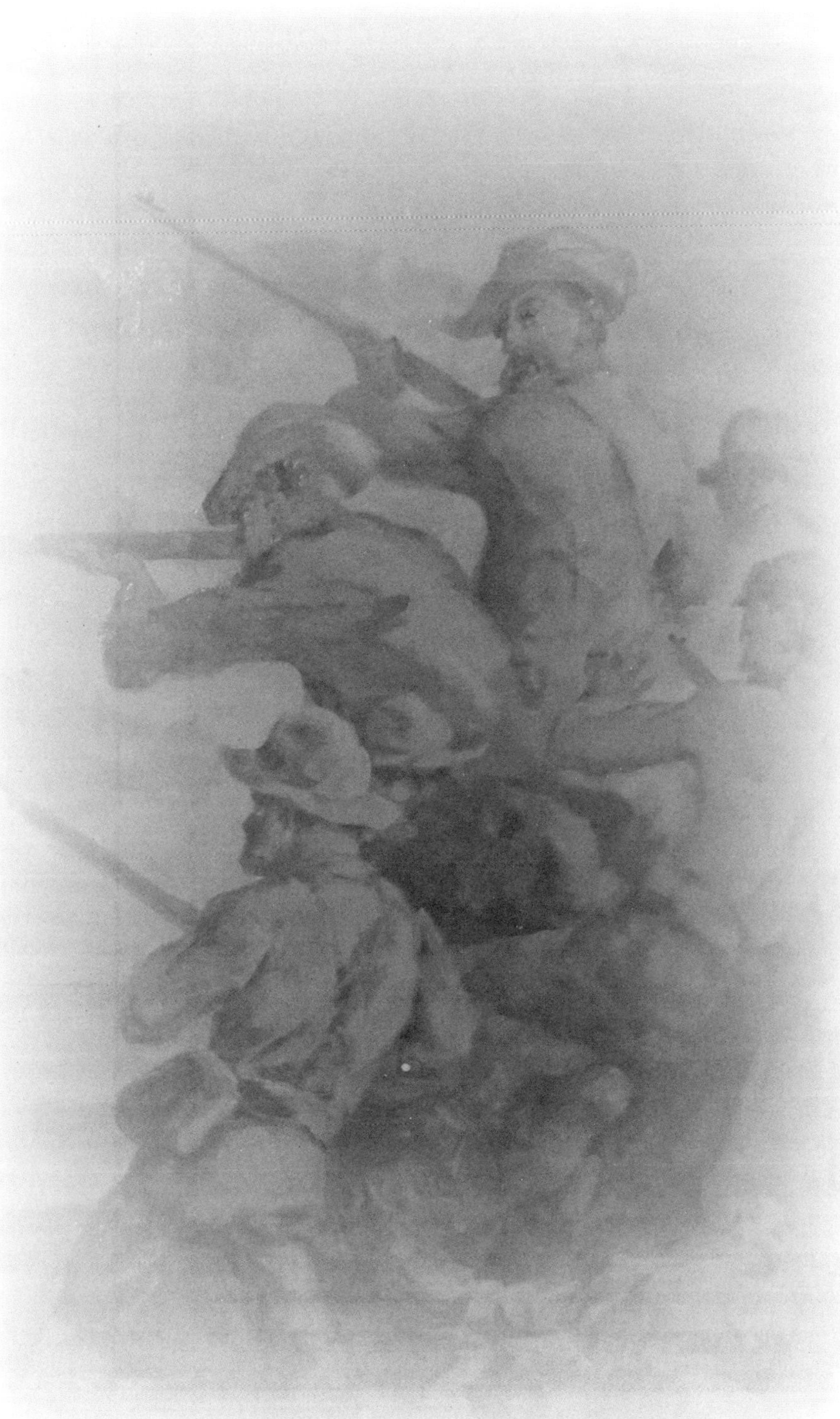

Contents

Foreword 9

Introduction 11
    Ghostly Locations: What Was There Before?

Part One: *Spirits in Springfield, Missouri* 17
    Doling Park 17
    Colonial Hotel 20
    Fox Theater 22
    Fassnight Park 25
    Commercial Street 29
    Springfield Public Square 31
    Landers Theater 32
    Parkview High School 34
    Gillioz Theater 34
    Maple Park Cemetery 36
    Central High School 41
    Cox Medical Center North 42
    Abou Ben Adhem Shrine Mosque 43
    Greenlawn Memorial Gardens 44
    Pythian Castle 45
    The Phantom of Valley Water Mill 47
    Highway 13 48
    The Bobbing Heads of James River 48
    Phelps Grove Park 49
    The Ghost of Bud Isbell 49
    The Ghost of Martin Danforth 50
    Springfield Land Fill 50
    Haunted Old Railroad Yard and Tracks 51
    The Bluegrass Farm 53
    College Hauntings 56
    Springfield National Cemetery 61
    City Hall 64
    Public Library 66
    Other Springfield Sightings 67
        Barth's Clothing Store • Grant Beach Park • Shady Inn • The Grove • St. John's Hospital
        Ritter Springs Park • River Bluff Cave • Sequiota Park • The Streets of Springfield • The
        Smiling Black Priest • Zagonyi Park • U.S. Medical Center for Federal Prisoners

Part Two: *Something's Amiss in Aurora, Missouri* 71
    Underwater Demons in the Mines 71
    Princess Theater 73

Contents

Part Three: *Barely There in Branson, Missouri* **75**
    The Hauntings... 75
    Branson Bits 78
        The Ghost of Cameron Mitchell • The Mists of White River

Part Four: *Chasing Ghosts in Chadwick, Missouri* **81**
    Bald Knobbers' Hanging Cave 81

Part Five: *Apparitions in Ash Grove, Missouri* **83**
    The Hauntings... 83
    The Haunted Bridge 83

Part Six: *Feeling the Spirits in Fair Grove, Missouri* **85**
    Ghost Bridge 85
    Haunted Highway 125 90

Part Seven: *"Spirited" St. Louis, Missouri* **91**
    The Hauntings... 92
    The Mississippi River 92
    Jefferson Barracks National Cemetery 93
    Haunted Caves 95
    Forest Park 97
    Hospital Spectors...& Other Ghostly Sites 98
        St. Louis Children's Hospital • Old City Hospital • Homer G. Phillips Hospital
        Adams-Gehm Haunted House • Lafayette Square

Part Eight: *Waking the Dead in Webster County* **101**
    Ghosts in the Rivers 101

Part Nine: *Fishing for Ghosts in Forsyth, Missouri* **103**
    Swan Creek Arch Bridge 103
        The Horseback Rider & Shadow Figures

Part Ten: *Ghostly Happenings in Galena, Missouri* **105**
    The Ghosts of Y-Bridge 105
    Green-Eyed Lady Ghost of Highway 248 105
    Another Dead Woman...Picture Found in Bible 108

Part Eleven: *Haunted Hannibal, Missouri* **111**
    The Hauntings... 111

Part Twelve: *Mystic Monett, Missouri* **113**
    The Ghost of Robert Mitchum 113
    The Gillioz Theater 114

Contents

Part Thirteen: *Spectors in St. Charles, Missouri* **115**
    The Hauntings... 115
    On the River 116
        Haunted Steamboat • Missouri River

Part Fourteen: *Seeing things in St. Genevieve, Missouri* **117**
    Haunted Houses, Taverns and Cemeteries 118
        Augustin Aubuchon - Therese Lalumondiere House • Beauvais - Amoureux House Bequette - Ribault House • Bolduc - Le Meilleur House • Guibord - Valle House • Jean Baptiste Valle House • Greentree Tavern • Labruyere House • St. Genevieve Memorial Cemetery

Part Fifteen: *Jousting the Spirits in Joplin, Missouri* **121**
    The Hauntings... 121
    The Ghost of Billy the Kid 123
    Joplin Hotspots 124
        Connor Hotel • Fox Theater • Joplin Supply Company • Schifferdecker Home Shoal Creek • Wildcat Glades Park

Part Sixteen: *Haunted Kansas City, Missouri* **127**
    The Hauntings... 127
    Christian Church Hospital 128
    Other Ghostly Hotspots 130
        Crown Center • Elwood Cemetery • Penn Valley Park • Swope Park • Union Cemetery • Union Station • Houston Lake

Part Seventeen: *Haunted Noel, Missouri* **135**
    Bluff Dwellers Cave 136

Part Eighteen: *Ghosts are Everywhere* **137**
        St. Robert, Missouri • Paris, Missouri • Shelbina, Missouri • Mexico, Missouri • St. James, Missouri • Salem, Missouri • Licking, Missouri • Cabool, Missouri • West Plains, Missouri • Mountain Grove, Missouri • Thayer, Missouri • Doniphan, Missouri • Poplar Bluff, Missouri • Carthage, Missouri • Stone County, Missouri • Nevada, Missouri • Warrensburg, Missouri • Knob Noster, Missouri • Sedalia, Missouri • Boonville, Missouri • Fayette, Missouri • Moberly, Missouri • St. Joseph, Missouri • Lake Pomme de Terre, Missouri • Possum Trot, Missouri • Bolivar, Missouri

Part Nineteen: *The Dead and Beyond* **151**
        Uneasy Spirits of Woodlock Cemetery, Davisville, Missouri • The Walking Dead of Wheeler Cemetery, Dixon, Missouri • Ghosts in the Morgue, Mount Vernon, Missouri • Deadman's Pond, Reeds Springs, Missouri • Cemetery Screamers, Windyville, Missouri

Contents

Part Twenty: *And Other Ghostly Tales* **155**

The Ghost of Alf Bolin, Ozark, Missouri • Indian Ghost Cave, Cassville, Missouri • Cry of the Banshee at Devil's Elbow, Missouri • The Ghost of Wyatt Earp, Lamar, Missouri • Witch Ghosts • The Weeping Woman, Hollister, Missouri • Spook Light Mystery, Hornet, Missouri • John Nelson Hanging, Palmyra, Missouri • Headless Union Soldier, Lebanon, Missouri • Captain William Anderson, Richmond, Missouri • The Ghost of Al Capone, Rockaway Beach, Missouri • The White Ghost Horse, Sparta, Missouri • Ghost Diver, Roubidoux Spring Cave, Waynesville, Missouri • Haunted Bandstand, Stotts City, Missouri • Black Female Hangings • Ghost Waitress, Marceline, Missouri • Outlaw Ghosts • The Ghosts of Wilson Creek National Battlefield • American Civil War Ghost Sites • French Ghosts • Ghost Towns and Underwater Cemeteries

Ghost Hunting Tips **173**

Getting There, Being There & Making Personal Discoveries • Internet Resources • Musings from the Midnight Hour

Suggested Readings **177**

Index **185**

Foreword

There's an argument that many skeptics make in regard to ghostly phenomena: "If this stuff is real, then show me!" Show me. There have been many occasions when I wish I could find a haunting so profound and so regular in occurrence that I could take a group of hard-nosed skeptics and say, "See! There it is." Alas, when it comes to ghosts, hauntings, and the supernatural, there are no rules and very little you can count on. But yet, the ghostly reports continue to pour in from all over the world and by people from all walks of life. The ghosts are here, and if you speak with Lee Prosser, you'll know the ghosts are in Missouri en force.

Lee is a Sensitive. That means he can pick up on subtleties that many of us can't quite see or feel. Lee says to the ghosts, "Show me," and they do. You might say he has a nose for haunts.

There is much discussion in the paranormal community as to what exactly a ghost is. Lee understands that a ghost can be many things. It can be that feeling or imprint leftover in a location from long ago, it can be a specter that still lurks around a building, and it can be someone's essence coming back for unfinished business.

What you're about to embark on is a ghostly tour of Missouri. Lee has put together a comprehensive directory of the haunts that make his state something special for fans of the paranormal and the unseen. From ghostly horses to haunted rivers, from spooky cemeteries to the ghost of Billy the Kid himself, *Missouri Hauntings* is full of adventures — and a supernatural tour of one of America's most haunted states. In addition to a historical overview of each setting, you'll benefit from Lee's insight and psychic sensitivity to delve deeper into the haunt. The legends and lore come alive when you walk by Shoal Creek in Joplin, the Homer G. Phillips Hospital in St. Louis, or the Haunted Steamboat in St. Charles. We may not be able to trap a ghost in a jar just yet, but tagging along with Lee Prosser on his ghostly adventures may just be the next best thing.

You should consider *Missouri Hauntings* a starting point. To fully appreciate the haunts and history, get out there and visit these locations for yourself. Find out what you feel, hear, and see when you walk by Bluff Dwellers Cave in Noel, or Deadman's Pond in Reeds Springs. There are ghosts in Missouri, and Lee Prosser will show you. Just turn the page.

Supernaturally yours,

Jeff Belanger
Founder of Ghostvillage.com
and author of The World's Most Haunted Places

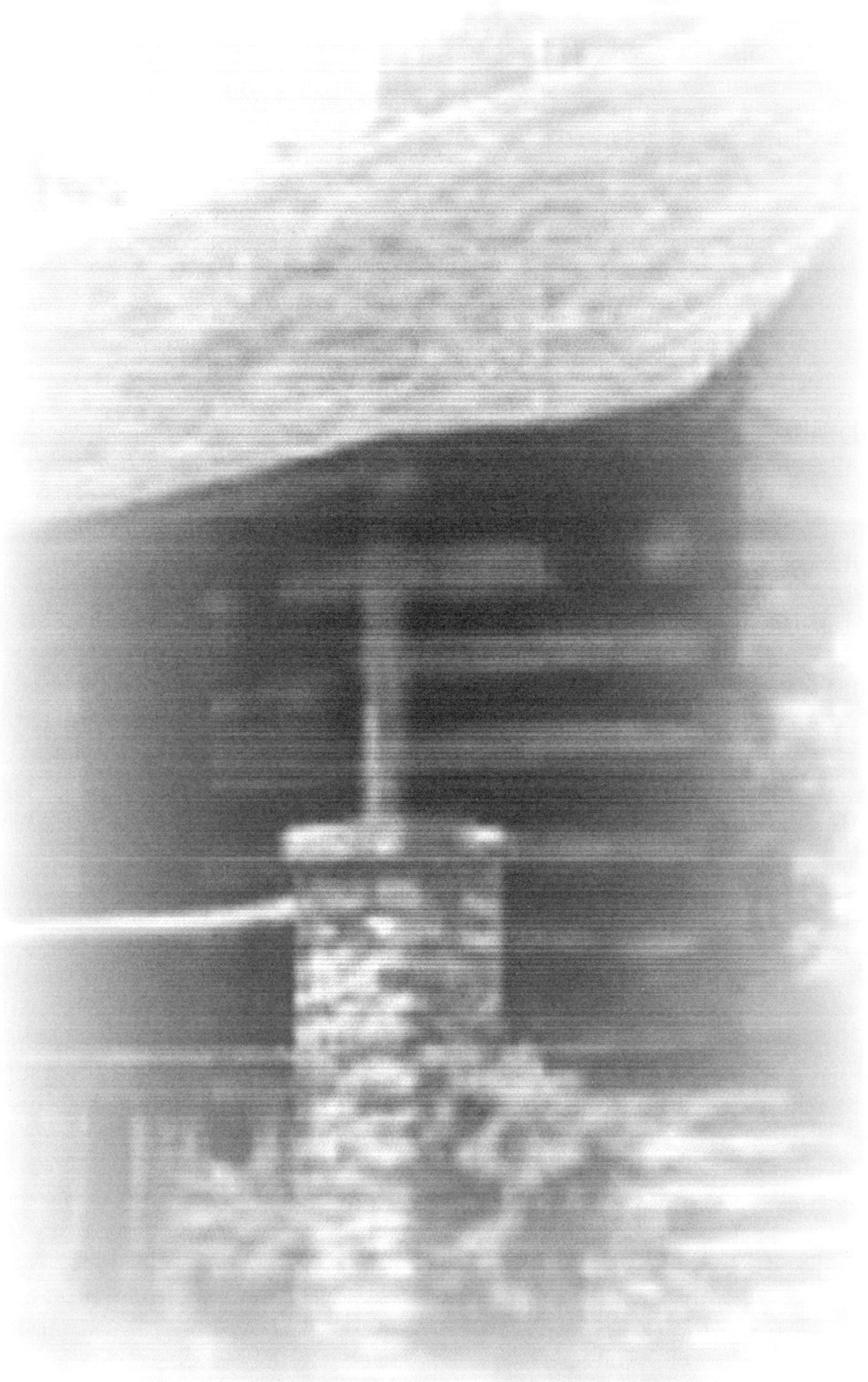

Introduction

I have lived in Missouri most of my life—and it has **ALWAYS** been haunted. In every home I have lived or visited I have *SEEN*, or *FELT*, the haunting presence. My wife Debra is sensitive to ghostly presences, too. In our home we have a ghost cat that interacts with not only us but with our living cats and dogs. We have a residual haunting of a little old lady going about her daily routine in the kitchen.

I own an old oil painting, done by a French artist and painted in Nimes, France, that is haunted. Something – a positive spirit – has attached itself to the cloth canvas and calls itself "Marie." This enchanted, original oil painting is hanging on the wall of our den. The image of this young woman's inquisitive dark, green-tinged eyes remains with you long after you have passed from the room. Marie's mischievous face is one not easily forgotten.

My Missouri, the place of my birth and upbringing, is one of the most haunted states in the United States. There are thousands of hauntings in Missouri and each has its own story to share. There are over 1,500 known caves in Missouri and most of them, too, have stories relating to ghostly phenomena.

There are several reasons for these hauntings, including: Missouri's historical place in opening the American Western Frontier; some of the bloodiest battles were fought here during the American Civil War; the state's location as a connection point to other states; the worldwide flu epidemic that struck the United States during World War I; connections with the American gangster era of the 1920s and 1930s; and legends/folklore of the American Indians and other ethnic groups. Missouri is a ghost-filled state.

For the purposes of reference, let me share with you some terms. *Essentially, there are two kinds of hauntings: intelligent and residual.* An **intelligent haunting** is where the ghost is trying to make contact. A **residual haunting** is a ghost stuck in time repeating an action, unaware of a human presence.

In many instances, a ghost may attach itself to an object. The object could be anything, such as a bed, book, camera, mirror, painting, drawing, boat, musical instrument, postcard, finger or toe rings, barn, motorcycle, rock, radio, pencil, silverware, eating utensils, glass, cave, photograph, gun, land, house, road, knife, pathway, automobile, key, or tree.

During a conversation with a friend in 2008, I asked her how many words are there for the word "ghost" and she told me the total was over 2,500 in different languages. *Well, here is a reference list of some words for the word "ghost":* apparition, spirit, phantom, specter, shade, wraith, revenant, and spook. Those are the most common words associated with the word "ghost"

Introduction

Marie.

and the words oftentimes used instead of "ghost." It depends on who is doing the name-calling!

Not all people see the same ghost at the same time. The ghost may appear to one person at one time in a given location, yet might not appear to a different person at the same place. Two people may see the ghost at the same time. Two people may be together and only one sees the ghost. Two people may be in a haunted situation and see nothing. It depends on what type of haunting it is, what type of variation within the haunting situation it is, the sensitivity and personality of the person involved, and the ghost. There are many factors that come into play when seeing a ghost. Just because a structure has been replaced with something new does not mean the ghosts or ghosts are gone because they can still haunt the land on which the original structure once stood! Yes, land itself can be haunted.

Given the nature of modern physics research, some sightings may be like looking at a slice of historical time, in which a scene is viewed by way of a wormhole that can open a portal between two different points in time.

Also, there is the actual paranormal energy involved. You have to consider what the unifying matter is within that dark or light energy that gives it paranormal universality. This applies whenever you examine a haunting involving shadow or full image appearances of something considered ghostly. Some matter and some energy have more light than others. This particular aspect offers many possibilities, and raises more questions than our current science of physics is able to offer satisfying answers to!

Another point to ponder is the numerous sightings throughout the world and the ghostly activity on highways, roads, old established trails, and pathways. Caves, homes, buildings, abandoned structures, historical sites, and cemeteries are other areas where hauntings frequently occur.

There are always accounts of what is known as *shadow figures*. **Shadow figures** are simply that, whereas one may have more detail and substance than another, they are usually gone as quickly as they arrive. There are instances where shadow figures do linger. A shadow figure may be either human or animal.

Every haunting does not have to have a cold spot, a hot spot, or chills running up and down your neck and spine. In fact, in many hauntings none of those things take place.

The purpose of this book is not to debunk or disprove ghosts, nor is it my intention or wish to prove the existence of ghosts. The purpose is to identify areas of Missouri hauntings based on available findings. I relied on my personal knowledge of the locations, my memories, and what people have verbally shared with me about a given area. I also relied on my sensitive perspective towards paranormal happenings, past and present.

But just because I might not sense a paranormal or haunting situation, or a ghost, when investigating an area does not mean it didn't happen or it's not happening.

As for being a sensitive, it's my belief that any person is capable of becoming a sensitive with time, training, and intuition. I have a theory on paranormal activity: *Paranormal activity is a form of existential reality based on pre-existing sequences in time.*

There is much literature about the paranormal, hauntings, and ghosts now available, so I urge you to read everything you can on the subject! Enjoy and think about what you discover. Analyze what you read and are told, and ask yourself if you have had similar things happen in your personal life or know about it happening in the life of another person. Then go out and discover what you personally find in face-to-face encounters!

Paranormal encounters have been happening to humans since the beginning of time. These occurrences are more openly talked about and revealed today than in the past because they are becoming more common and more widespread. Different cultures define paranormal occurrences differently, and should be analyzed in the context of the times in which they took place.

Develop your latent sensitive talents and train your intuition to work flawlessly for you. It can, and it will.

For now, it's time to go visiting! Come join me on the trail of Missouri hauntings! Let us begin our journey in the city of Springfield, which started out as a small Southern town founded in the year 1830, blessed with an abundance of Southern customs and attitudes, Ozark hill country traditions, grit, adventure, spirit, friendliness, and the tenacity to survive. By the year 2008, that small Southern town had grown into a prosperous, friendly metropolis with a metropolitan area population of over 326,000 people. Springfield is the third largest city in Missouri, and is affectionately known as the heart and soul of the Missouri Ozarks by its residents.

Ghostly Locations: What Was There Before?

If you come upon a cleared area, and your feeling is that it's haunted and has some spirit activity, maybe it does. What would be most helpful in such a search where there may no longer be structures or landmarks of any kind is to check the land itself. You can do this by going to any public library and looking at documented images of the area in question, which are usually identified in Sanborn Maps, or other documentations. For instance, I was investigating the many theater locations no longer in existence on Commercial Street in Springfield. After a careful search, I found them in the Sanborn Maps. Find the city, and when required, the county, and start looking. I found the precise appearance of the building structures in the Sanborn Maps, Springfield, Missouri, Volume 2, number 203, year 1933.

Just because an area that once contained a structure is now vacant and empty does not mean anything to a ghost still lingering there! That ghost is still there, for time is meaningless to ghosts in their dimension!

When thinking about unusual ghostly locations, don't forget to consider what lies beneath the water. Water hides lots of things resting under silt and sand and mud! The waves may lap up against a gentle beach along a lake or rock outcropping by a river in the woods, but once upon a time there may have been something there. Did a small town once exist there where people laughed, walked, made love, argued, were born and died now covered by water, or perhaps a military battle site now covered by the cool water? What has come to settle at the bottom of these recent human-made lakes? What ghostly things lay sleeping in those murky depths awaiting re-discovery? For those interested in underwater exploration, such maps and other documentation could shed light on lost towns, caves, mines, and happenings now underwater. Maps lead to all kinds of interesting discoveries and possibilities for research.

I have several travel road maps of the state of Missouri, each one listing towns that no longer exist; the oldest map is dated 1934. It's amazing what information is found in old maps! When I lived in Roswell, New Mexico with my wife Debra, we had several old travel road maps of the state, and it was an enjoyable outing to follow where old railroad lines had once been leading to small towns that had once been. The same applies to Missouri or any state — there is always something just around the corner to discover, visit, and explore. There are ghost towns to be discovered, somewhere. A helpful suggestion for all potential ghost hunters is this: *When you come across an old state or county map at a garage sale or elsewhere, purchase it quickly! Examine the map and enjoy what you discover. Then, put that map to use, visit with people in the area you will be in and see what ghost stories they may recall and wish to share, take notes, and go exploring!*

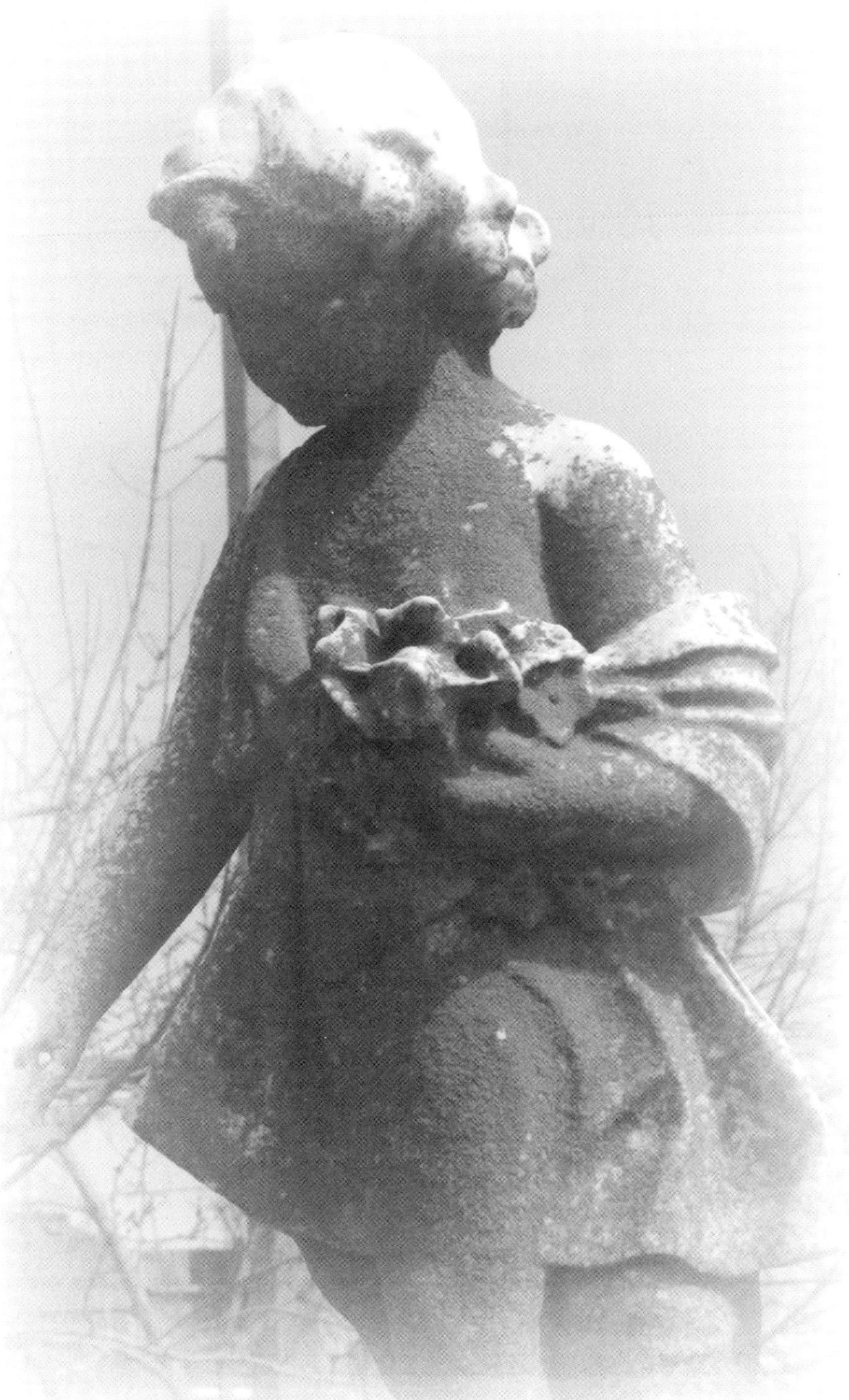

1

Spirits in Springfield, Missouri

Doling Park

Springfield is one of the most haunted cities in the state of Missouri. Doling Park, located near the intersection of Campbell and Talmage Streets in northern Springfield, is one place that has had its share of hauntings and apparitions.

Giboney Cave is located in the park and belonged to John Thomas and James Giboney. The Giboney Brothers purchased the forty-acre track of land and settled it in 1846. The park was later named for James Marshall Doling, a wealthy merchant who helped develop and build up North Springfield. Doling purchased the land from the Giboney brothers in 1882 and later turned the area into a park with his son, Robert.

The land was sold again, this time to the Springfield Amusement Company in 1907. The park was developed and at one time had several attractions, including a dance hall, penny arcade, two bandstands, roller coaster, a funhouse with a mechanical gypsy lady named Gertie, skating rink, merry-go-round, and a large theater. Gertie is well remembered for her loud laugh! I can still hear her strange laughter reaching out to me across the decades!

Tours of Giboney Cave were available by boat to see its six-foot high waterfall inside. Doling Park became known as the Queen of the Parks in Springfield, and its heyday was approximately 1907 to 1929. A large white wooden bridge with canoeing and boating were two of its many charms.

The Pavilion on the shore of Doling Lake also contained a ladies bathhouse, and on the second floor of this structure was the movie theater. The skating rink, known as the roller rink, was built in 1929 on the original site of the Giboney cabin. Johnny Kemm was among the many organists who performed for patrons as skaters of all ages skated on a hardwood maple floor. I spent many a fine time roller-skating on this old floor of the rink, and I know there were ghost skaters there, too...ghosts from other eras. I wonder where those haunted planks of wood went to and what

Doling Park entrance.

became of them? What a story each board could tell by touching it! I recall fond memories of the penny arcade and the funhouse.

One of the most popular amusement rides was Shoot-the-Chutes. There was an icehouse where ice was cut from the frozen lake in the winter and then stored in the icehouse for summer use.

In 1929, the land was sold to the city of Springfield. In the 1970s, the last of the ride attractions were removed. In the 1980s, the roller rink was turned into the Northview Community Center.

The sites where these historical structures once stood carry their own ghosts. The funhouse area is said to have ghosts, and apparitions have been seen near the Northview Community Center. Laughter has been heard in the area where the penny arcade and funhouse once stood. Muted sounds of a band playing have been heard in the wind on warm summer nights.

Giboney Cave itself is full of macabre happenings that date back over a 200-year period, and although not fully explored, the cave does connect under the Springfield Public Square some miles away. The cave entrance is blocked from public access, but people are able to walk up to the cave passage and look directly into its murky depths.

Stories abound about this area and its strange cave. There is the story of a young couple, who, in 1925, went into the cave exploring and disappeared, never to be heard from again. Their ghosts are said to haunt the depths of the cave. A young man ventured into the cave in 1940 and

Cave entrance with stream from cave.

Main cave entrance.

never returned. Ghosts of soldiers from both World Wars have said to be seen. Ghosts of American Indians have been seen near the cave entrance. At twilight, figure shadows are sometimes discerned in the immediate area of the cave and near the lake facing the cave.

I talked with a woman who said she had her right breast firmly squeezed while waiting for a ride from a friend. She was standing close to the entrance drive by Doling Park when she had her ghostly encounter in 2008. She said at the time of this visit by the invisible presence, she did not know whether to be scared or mad, or both, and was both!

Walking through this lovely park in the daytime is an enjoyable journey, and watching the geese and ducks in the lake is an amusement in itself. There is a feeling of time and history in this park, and you can receive a sense of it by simply sitting down on one of the park benches, relaxing, and observing. Doling Park, once the hub for visitors from all over the state of Missouri and elsewhere to experience and enjoy, still maintains its unique charm. When you visit, you will get a good sense of its timeless history.

Colonial Hotel

205 South Jefferson Avenue

The Colonial Hotel was once one of the finest hotels in downtown Springfield. Located at 205 South Jefferson Avenue, it was ideally suited for those passing through on personal or business visits, and for living accommodations. Various celebrities and well-known politicians often stayed there for lodging. Among them were President Truman and John F. Kennedy. Elvis Presley stayed at the Colonial Hotel during his first trip to Springfield, Missouri in the 1950s.

A brick building with steel reinforcement, the hotel was six stories high. The building was built in 1907 and had two hundred rooms, a coffee shop, and a cocktail lounge. Charles Sansone, owner of the Sansone Hotel, purchased the Colonial Hotel from John Landers and his son, D. J. Landers, in 1925. John Landers purchased the hotel again in 1962. In 1963, Ward Chrisman purchased the hotel. Due to changing times and the closing of Business Route 66, by 1978 the building was empty and an end was at hand for this landmark hotel in Southwest Missouri.

In 1986, Ward Chrisman donated the old hotel to the Southwest Missouri State University Foundation. The end for the historic building came in late 1997 when it was demolished and its rubble removed to make room for a new university parking lot. I have been in the Colonial Hotel many times. It was an interesting place. The lounge always seemed to me to have shadows moving about, reminding me of that old phrase about things that go bump in the night.

Old vintage postcard of Colonial Hotel.

There are many ghost stories surrounding the Colonial Hotel. A young woman dressed in blue, 1940s clothes, walking the third floor, alone and waiting for her lover, was seen to vanish into a room near the right of the hallway. An elderly couple dressed in 1930s clothing was seen in the middle section on the second floor. Two sailors on leave during World War II were seen staring from a third floor window that overlooked Jefferson Avenue. A young boy on the ground floor dressed in 1920s-style clothes, tossing a baseball in the air, would disappear laughing around a corner on the first floor...the laughter ending abruptly. Three attractive women dressed in 1940s clothes were observed laughing together and sitting at a table in the lounge. An elderly, well-dressed man appeared in the men's restroom during the early 1950s, but would vanish when approached. Strange glows or orbs on the second floor were seen for years during the winter months. During the early 1950s, there was a young couple wearing clothes in the style of the 1930s seen on the fifth floor in the western section of the hotel. An elderly woman dressed in 1920s clothing was seen on the fifth floor of the western section of the hotel. A petite blonde-haired woman wearing a prom dress possibly from the early 1960s, seen at the lounge entrance talking with two young men dressed in prom clothes of the same era, vanished upon being approached by a group going into the lounge.

Fox Theater

The building that was once the Fox Theater is located in Springfield Public Square. The Fox Theater opened in 1916. Many people have said it is built on an entrance to the cave running to and connecting with Doling Park. I recall my Uncle Willard telling me that there was a bank vault in the basement of the theater that contained European paintings from the 1930s era, and was actually built into the cave opening and used to seal the cave's entrance. Uncle Willard did not allow me to sit in the balcony because he believed it was not a good place to be. There have been stories of ghostly presences in the basement and the balcony. Located on the northeast corner of the Springfield Public Square, it remains a fine personal memory to me, for as a child I went to see many movies at the Fox Theater.

I recall going to a Saturday showing and the western cowboy actor Randolph Scott was there. Randolph Scott (1898–1987) was a fine actor from North Carolina who was also a Freemason and active in the York Rite. Among his classic movies were such films as "The Virginian" (1929), "Supernatural" (1933), "Roberta" (1935), "She" (1935), "Seven Men from Now" (1955), "Tall T" (1956), and "Ride the High Country" (1962). I remember seeing Scott on stage and hearing him speak to the happy, loud audience. Later, I shook his hand in the theater lobby in front of the wall murals.

American Civil War wall mural.

Part One: Spirits in Springfield, Missouri

Lee Prosser standing where as a child he shook the hand of actor Randolph Scott.

Lee and Debra Prosser at wall murals in lobby of the Fox Theater.

These wall murals are registered historic landmarks, and I remember shaking Scott's hand in front of the mural depicting the American Civil War battle at Wilson's Creek.

While living in Santa Monica Canyon, California during the 1960s, I came into contact again with Randolph Scott, who was attending a movie with fellow actor Wendell Corey (1914–1968). I went up to him, re-introduced myself and shook his hand again. I told him I was living in Santa Monica Canyon not far from the home of my friends, novelist Christopher Isherwood and his companion, artist Don Bachardy. Scott and I visited and then went our separate ways. Randolph Scott was truly one of the most gracious, polite people you could ever hope to encounter; he had a sense of Southern class about him that was impeccable. His voice, smile, and handshake were sincere. Randolph Scott made some of the finest American Western films in movie history. He may still be visiting the Fox Theater at some ghostly matinee!

Today, the Fox Theater is a pleasant church setting owned by the Abundant Life Covenant Church. This positive, enjoyable religious setting is a nice place to attend services, and they publish their own religious magazine titled *Present Truth*.

Debra and I both felt the gentle peacefulness of this religious setting, and we both had the good fortune of encountering numerous scenes from past events that took place in the large auditorium and on its stage.

The stage had psychic images of a positive nature that Debra and I both witnessed, comfortably. These were definitely residual images, and more along the lines of a history tour with the psychic images from the past marching along at a fast clip. One particular scene Debra and I both shared was the psychic image of the theater seats being filled with children intently watching a movie on the screen!

The original J.C. Penney building was located next to the Fox Theater, as was a clothing store named Barth's. Among contemporary ghost hunters, this corner of the Square is considered extremely haunted.

Rumors of ghostly encounters and cold spots in the bathrooms, basement, and other areas of the old J.C. Penny building have been rampant over the years. Nothing harmful has ever taken place, but rather people having encounters with presences, sounds, and voices.

Fassnight Park

Llocated at Meadowmere and South Campbell Streets next to Parkview High School.

Fassnight Park with Parkview High School in background on hill.

Conrad and Emma Fassnight sold twenty-eight acres of land in 1924 to the city of Springfield. This land included trees and a creek. Over a period of years, under the direction and guidance of a stonemason named Godfrey Messerli, the Works Progress Administration completed the bathhouse, pool, bridges, and other structures as part of a project. In 1977, the pool and structures were renovated.

A persistent story since the 1930s was that there existed small openings to caves in the Fassnight Park bluffs and that they were dynamited to seal these entrances off, to keep children from entering them. My examination of these rock formations revealed to me that there could have been such cave openings and the openings were collapsed. With the passage of time, fact mixes with rumor and it becomes difficult to ascertain if there were cave openings. Given the nature of the Missouri cave system and its many connections, it's very possible the cave openings were a fact. As a child I played and went swimming in this park often.

The bathhouse is considered haunted. There have been ghost stories over the years of swimmers entering the bathhouse, seeing another person there, and then that person is suddenly gone.

Three other ghost stories of merit should also be noted. One is the appearance of a young, dark-haired woman wearing a short purple dress during the twilight hours; she is leaning over the metal fence railing at the top of the stairs, looking down at the park.

Another haunting is that of a young man wearing a black swimsuit looking out from the bathhouse balcony across the swimming pool. An elderly woman dressed in 1940s clothes is reputed to be waving at some person in the park from her vantage point at the top of the stairs; she is facing the left bridge. An interesting aspect of these residual hauntings is their quick appearance and disappearance — and the fact that different people have seen different things over the decades.

Shadow figures have also been seen near the bathhouse...they vanish when approached. Peals of rowdy laughter have been heard inside the bathhouse when nobody is there.

Two young women in love, strolling hand in hand, have been seen crossing the bridge...they walk over the bridge and vanish at the other end. This couple is seen during the early winter months. They are wearing long coats, dressed for cool weather, and wearing stocking caps. Age wise, they appear to be in their early thirties. They show no recognition of the living as they peacefully stroll together. The appearance of these two women ghosts is that of a residual haunting.

I personally spent a lot of time in this old park, and I am aware of its enduring charm and haunted nature. I have seen the ghost of the young woman wearing a short purple dress.

Fassnight pavilion snow-covered steps.

Full view of Fassnight Park pavilion.

Bridge over Fassnight Park.

Commercial Street

Over a period of decades, North Springfield has had its share of hauntings. Commercial Street was once home to movie theaters, hotels, restaurants, and many businesses in its heyday. It was a prosperous business section of Springfield where people could get a good meal, see a movie, shop, and purchase groceries. For a few years, North Springfield was its own city. Some of its businesses included the Diemer Theater, Commercial Club of Springfield Community Center, Springfield Motor Sales, Rathbone Hardware, Lyons Grocer and Feed Store, and the Milner Hotel. Since 2008, the buildings on Commercial Street have been gradually restored.

Walking on either side of Commercial Street, from approximately where it borders Campbell Avenue to Washington Avenue, you get a feel and glimpse of what it had been like in the 1900s or earlier.

To walk an area is always preferable. Whenever feasible, depending upon the circumstances, I would recommend to a person wanting to explore haunted areas or write about ghostly things, to first walk that area and see what feelings come to her or him. Follow your intuition.

During the late 1930s there was a movie theater at 406 East Commercial Avenue called the Granada Theater. A man was found dead in an alleyway close to this theater and was reputed to haunt the theater thereafter.

Commercial Street.

Part One: Spirits in Springfield, Missouri

Standing on the Jefferson Street Footbridge.

There were at least three theaters from 303 to 314 Commerce; they were next to an awning factory and tin shop at 315 and a wholesale grocer at 317 East Commercial. On the other side of the street were more businesses and hotels.

There is an old building that served as a bookstore for two different owners over several decades. This bookstore is a two-story brick building. A young woman's ghost has been seen in the upstairs front windows. She is wearing a red lacy dress, much like those seen in the 1880s to about 1900, has auburn hair, fair-complexioned, and she is staring innocently out the window with a friendly smile on her face. Whether she is enjoying the moment in time as simply that or excited over something having been said directly behind her, is anybody's guess. The building does not have an entrance stairway to the second floor rooms. There may be other ghostly occupants there as yet unknown. The basement, also sealed up, contains a strange tunnel that meanders about, disappearing into the darkness. What went on in the dark basement and in that tunnel are questions unanswered at this time, but it's something to think and wonder about. Who was the young woman in the red lacy dress? What is her history, and what became of her? There are questions, but no answers about her identity.

Entrance to Jefferson Street Footbridge.

I last visited the bookstore in 2004 and purchased nice copies with dust jackets of John Master's novel, *Bhowani Junction,* and Christopher Isherwood's novel, *Down There on a Visit.* At that time, the upstairs and basement entrances were still sealed up. Passing by the building in 2008, the bookstore is gone and the building is closed and empty.

Ghosts and shadow figures have also been seen on the old Jefferson Street Footbridge that crosses over the train tracks. What fluke of time allows them to continue their strolls across this old footbridge built in 1902? Who were they?

There is much history in these old Commercial Street buildings, and the ongoing renovations will only add to that history. Stroll the street on both sides and feel its history. You will find it an interesting experience. Remember what you see!

Springfield Public Square

The Square, as old-time residents affectionately call it, has a checkered history that is both interesting and important. It's haunted by paranormal activity and ghosts that date back to the 1800s. With the passage of time and such events as hangings, war, murders, unexplained deaths, and gunfights taking place, the Springfield Public Square has grown in stature as a haunted location.

John Polk Campbell donated the acreage for the Public Square in 1835 and the first courthouse was built in the center section of this Square. During 1858 the Butterfield Overland Stage established a stop point route there.

As the American Civil War got underway, the state was torn between North and South control. Colonel Franz Sigel, with his Union troops, arrived at the Square on June 24, 1861, and troops extended their excursions into North Springfield. By August, Confederate soldiers, led by General Sterling Price, seized control of the Square. On October 25, 1861, a skillful raid by Union troops under the command of Major Charles Zagonyi resulted in the burning and destruction of the Square courthouse. During 1862 and 1863 both the North and South attempted to secure Springfield for its own use. Confederate forces were overcome and driven back by Union soldiers on January 8, 1863.

The Square continues its importance as a historical hub for Springfieldians, and in 1970 the area was named Park Central Square. Much of the Square has been renovated and the old buildings refurbished.

One interesting building on the Public Square is the seven-story Heer's store, which was originally built in 1869. Constructed for use as a department store, it was solidly built with steel, terra cotta, wood, and concrete. It had 100,000 feet of usable floor space. Ravaged by fire, it was rebuilt in 1915. The Heer's building had a long, prosperous life until it went out of business in 1995. Heer's, as a landmark structure, continues to be restored as of 2009.

There are other old buildings on the Public Square and in the immediate surrounding area, including the Holland Building and the Woodruff Building. Visitors to the Springfield Public Square will find it fascinating.

Landers Theater

311 East Walnut Street, in the Springfield Public Square area

Originally constructed in 1907, the Landers building served many theatrical purposes. There were times when the theater was closed during its long history. A despondent stagehand is said to have hanged himself from the roof and was not discovered until far into a performance taking place below his dangling body. He is said to haunt the building. Stories of lights mysteriously being turned on and off by ghostly presences have happened. Macabre laughter has been heard in the restrooms and balcony. Shadow figures have been seen in the restrooms.

Beautifully restored and renovated, Landers Theater is now home to the Springfield Little Theater, which gives live performances. This old theater has comfortable seating, a distinct sense of history, and a charming atmosphere about it.

Landers Theater.

Parkview High School.

Parkview High School

**516 North Meadowmere Street,
next to Fassnight Park.**

Parkview High School was built in 1959 and is located on a grass knoll off of North Meadowmere Street.

A young woman, completing her senior class year in 1963, was the victim of a drowning accident down in the lake country surrounding Springfield. Her ghost is seen intermittently in the halls of the school and near the school entrance by the parking lot facing Fassnight Park. She is looking for somebody, perhaps a school friend of her time.

But it's not just students roaming the halls in the afterlife. The ghost of a Parkview English teacher appears near the main offices between the hours of 5 and 7 p.m. She is smiling and is described as thin and petite.

Gillioz Theater

**317 Park Central,
in the Springfield Public Square**

Fully restored now, Gillioz Theater is an ornate and beautiful theater with a strong theatrical heritage.

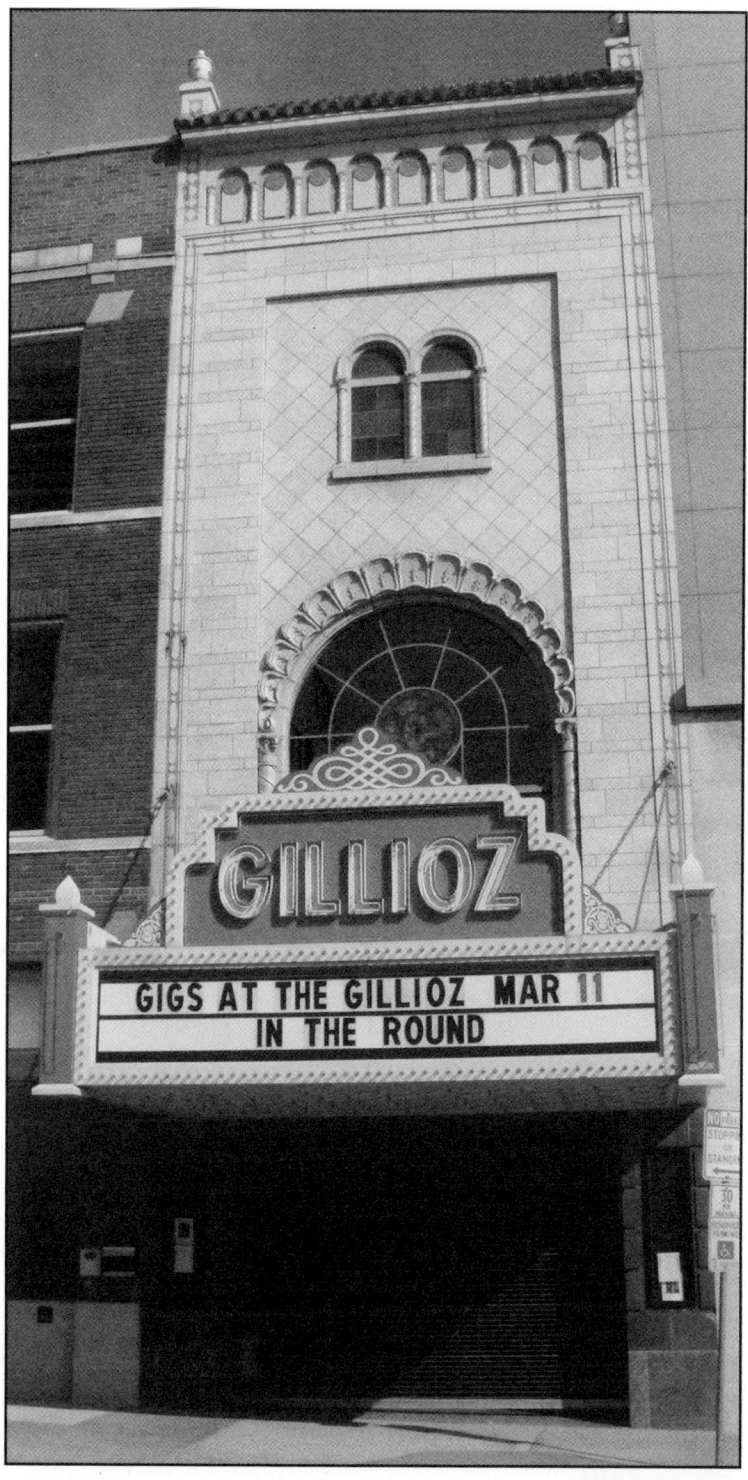

Gillioz Theater.

I recall a ghostly encounter in the men's restroom during December 1963. I was dating a young woman at the state college, and we went to a movie there along with some friends. I think the movie was "Dr. No" starring Sean Connery. I was in the process of washing my hands when a little boy around ten years old walked into the bathroom. He had a curious smile on his face, glanced at me, and then vanished into the adjacent wall. The little boy never reappeared...*JUST VANISHED*. There was an older man in the bathroom at the time. We looked at each other, both having seen this haunting, and he nodded and walked out without saying a word about the incident. I never encountered this curious little ghost again during the times I used this theater bathroom.

Maple Park Cemetery

300 West Grand Street

Maple Park Cemetery is one of the most natural and peaceful cemeteries anywhere, although it does have a haunted atmosphere about it. The cemetery has a certain charm and peacefulness about it as visitors walk its maple-lined driveways, finding the well-kept landscape enchanting. There is an Edwardian feel to some driveways, and depending on where you are walking, it's as if the cemetery is sharing different time eras with you.

The old Gazebo is an intriguing site, and has been restored to its original architectural design.

Of the numerous cemeteries I have investigated, Maple Park ranks high on my list of pleasant places to visit whether living or dead. My Uncle Willard loved the feeling of peacefulness he would get in this old cemetery. He loved it so much that he selected it for his final resting place rather than Greenlawn Memorial Gardens where a large chunk of my relatives are interned. Uncle Willard loved the maples in this cemetery and would often walk through the grounds during the spring and fall. I have walked the pathways often myself, and there is always something new to see and take notice of.

Opened in 1876, this cemetery contains the bodies of many notable Springfield residents. One of special interest is Dave Tutt, who was killed during a gun duel with Wild Bill Hickok on the Springfield Public Square July 21, 1863. The gun duel was fought over a poker debt dispute involving Wild Bill Hickok's watch.

Dave Tutt's body was buried elsewhere and then moved to Maple Park in 1890. Sightings of a shadow figure, credited with being the restless ghost of Dave Tutt, have been seen near the grave.

The ghostly figure of a little girl has also been seen in the summer playing around an old concrete statue of a pensive child. I have seen her,

Old gazebo in Maple Park Cemetery.

Grave marker of Willard David Firestone.

Maple Park Cemetery mausoleums.

Part One: Spirits in Springfield, Missouri

Pensive child statue.

Marble statue of Angel.

and she is aware of human contact. I would say she appears to different people for different reasons.

And, ghostly figures have been seen around two aboveground burial mausoleums. Stories about such figures around old grave markers who vanish upon approach are not unusual.

The gazebo is said to be haunted with the sounds of a band playing on it, heard on windy days. Having stood on this old structure, nothing surprises me about it. Constructed with a saracenic architectural design, that old gazebo hides its macabre secrets well.

There is a very old marble statue of an angel in another section of the cemetery. It's said to have orbs around it at night.

There are many interesting statues, memorials, and cross markers in Maple Park Cemetery. It's a charming location and certainly worthy of a visit. Walk on its winding driveways, take some time to stand on the gazebo, close your eyes, feel the breeze...and *ENCOUNTER* something you had not anticipated in this ghostly cemetery.

Central High School

423 East Central Street

Built in 1893, Central High School is centrally located in the heart of Springfield not far from the original courthouse, and it has

Central High School.

a long, colorful history. It has had many graduating senior classes since its opening.

Orbs have been seen on different floors, and the attics and basements are also believed to be haunted.

The ghost of an elderly teacher wearing 1930s clothing has been seen in the old auditorium, but she vanishes when approached.

Shadow figures have been seen in the auditorium and hallways. And people have reported feelings of being watched near the restrooms, but no one is ever there...

Cox Medical Center North

1423 North Jefferson Avenue

One of the oldest hospitals in Springfield, Cox Hospital North is reputed to have had many hauntings, ghosts, and shadow figures within its structure, most notably on the sixth and seventh floors. Located on North Jefferson Avenue, it has a long and useful history as a medical setting. It was started in November 1906 due to the kind generosity of a woman named Ellen A. Burge, a devout Methodist. In 1908, the hospital was a three-story brick structure that housed thirty beds. The Burge School of Nursing was established in 1907 and in 1931 the hospital expanded in size. In 1962, the hospital was renamed the Burge-Protestant Hospital and renamed again in 1968 the Lester E. Cox Medical Center.

In 1981, it became Cox Medical Center North. The hospital has undergone many renovations and expansions since it was first founded.

Over the decades, there have been many sightings of ghosts and an abundance of shadow figures. There have been stories of voices being heard on the stairs and in the bathrooms and elevators.

Like with most hospitals, such hauntings are not unusual simply because hospitals are unique places in that they deal with pain, sorrow, joy, loss, hope, death, and survival on a daily basis. Given the age of this hospital, it has had time to accumulate a lot of psychic memories for hauntings of one type or another.

Contact between the living and the dead has been spoken of, but no definite records remain of these intelligent haunting situations—only stories passed on among family members or people visiting somebody in the hospital and encountering or seeing a ghost. Residual hauntings are most often spoken about. One story is that the hospital is built on land once occupied by American Indians in the late 1790s.

Abou Ben Adhem Shrine Mosque

601 East St. Louis Street

This five-story building was built in 1923 and is on the National Register of Historic Places. The design is arabesque and impressive to look at. It's located at 601 East St. Louis Street, not far from the Springfield Public Square downtown area.

There have been ghost sightings circulating about this unusual structure since the 1930s. It has a large auditorium, arena, and stage. Many live performances have taken place there over the decades, among them the Sara Evans concert on January 27, 2007.

The Shrine Mosque, as the community calls it, is a beautiful, well-kept structure. It's reputed to have a male ghost in the basement area and a second ghost of an older woman who haunts the fourth floor. The ghost of a young boy has been seen at times on the second and third floors.

Shrine Mosque.

Greenlawn Memorial Gardens

3506 North National Avenue

Greenlawn Memorial Gardens Cemetery is an old cemetery that contains a lot of buried history with its occupants. There are stories of hauntings, including ghostly figures seen at various grave markers.

I was told by different people not to ever visit this cemetery during the midnight hours. However, visiting it during the day was like taking a quiet, peaceful walk and I had an opportunity to see the magnificent Masonic Memorial. Nothing unusual came my way.

Masonic Memorial.

Part One: Spirits in Springfield, Missouri

I have found over the years that cemeteries oftentimes take on a special, different life in the night and dark morning hours, and that is when you have people talking about encountering paranormal activity. *Of course, shadow figures can appear in the day or night, anywhere, anytime.*

Pythian Castle

1451 East Pythian Street

Pythian Castle has been many things over the decades. It has a reputation as a place where both intelligent and residual hauntings occurring. Located at 1451 East Pythian Street, it has an imposing appearance. There are many stories that have flourished over the years about this unusual place, which was originally constructed by the Knights of Pythias as an orphanage in 1913. The Knights of Pythias was a charitable organization and much information is available about it, including material found on the Internet.

Later, the building and land was purchased by the United States military and used for German soldier internment during World War II. It's rumored that some of these prisoners of war were tortured during confinement and some died.

My first encounter with the haunted Pythian Castle was in 1956 when I went there with my Uncle Willard. I do not recall why we went there, but I recall vividly what happened to me. Inside the entrance, somebody touched my face—though I could not see anybody or anything to explain the touching. Then I heard a woman's gentle voice beside me, but I could see **NOTHING** and **NOBODY** except my Uncle Willard and I who were standing inside the entrance.

At the time of contact, I felt a sudden chill pass through me, but nothing else. That is all that I recall of the ghostly encounter, and it does remain a vivid, early memory of being part of a haunting.

Over its nearly hundred years of existence, ghostly experiences have been spoken about and passed on from one generation to another. *These hauntings include being touched by something not seen, bumping into a mass but not seeing anything, a mass bumping into a person or persons on its way to somewhere, an abundance of orbs, quick temperature changes, doors shutting by themselves, furniture moving by itself, a variety of children and adult voices heard, laughter, a woman weeping, a man weeping, strange mists that form and vanish, and the sound of a meowing cat running upstairs.*

A terrifying documentary was filmed about this building and other haunted places titled "Children of the Grave," by well-known filmmakers Philip Adrian Booth and Christopher Saint Booth. It was released as a DVD in 2007. Scary in the truest sense of the word, this documentary will have you sitting on the edge of your seat as you watch it unfold and wonder what horror is coming along next to confront you! There is much shocking

Pythian Castle.

ghost footage that will scare viewers with its intensity. Anybody wishing to see a ninety minute film version about some of Missouri's hauntings and scary places will find this a great item to own and view.

For those interested in an entertaining 1950s look at occurrences based on true paranormal events, take a look at the old black and white television series, "One Step Beyond" (1959–1961) with guest host John Newland. A new DVD release of the fifty best complete episodes was released in 2007 on a special four-CD collection. This popular series dramatized paranormal stories that were based on actual events and featured numerous actors and actresses including Christopher Lee, Elizabeth Montgomery, Mike Connors, Yvette Mimieux, Suzanne Pleshette, Ross Martin, Norma Crane, Robert Loggia, Joanne Linville, Charles Bronson, Albert Salmi, Patrick O'Neal, Peggy Ann Garner, Robert Webber, Louise Fletcher, Patrick

Macnee, Elen Willard, George Grizzard, Barbara Lord, Richard Devon, and Cloris Leachman.

There are also many movies available for watching, among them the critically-acclaimed "The Legend of Hell House" (1973) with Pamela Franklin, Roddy McDowall, Clive Revill, and Gayle Hunnicutt; "Stephen King's Rose Red" (2002) with Julian Sands, Nancy Travis, Matt Keeslar, and David Dukes; "The Shining" (1980) with Jack Nicholson and Shelly Duvall; "The Changeling" (1979) with George C. Scott and Trish Van Devere; "The Ghost Goes West" (1936) with Robert Donat and Jean Parker; "Ghostbusters" (1984) with Bill Murray, Dan Aykroyd, and Sigourney Weaver; "The Ghost and Mrs. Muir" (1947) with Rex Harrison and Gene Tierney; and "Ghost"" (1990) with Patrick Swayze and Demi Moore. Also, the popular television series "The Ghost Whisperer" (2005) is enjoyable viewing about ghosts and hauntings. Some of humankind's greatest fears about hauntings, ghosts, macabre incidents, paranormal occurrences, and the supernatural have been dramatized in film.

Fiction writers have capitalized on these fears for decades, and such writings are too many to list, but a few are *The Uninhabited House, Ghosts in Daylight, A Phantom Lover, Ghost Story, The Beckoning Fair One, Widdershins, The Turn of the Screw, A Christmas Carol, They Return at Evening*, and *The Lady in White*.

As long as humans feel fear and excitement about paranormal events, there will be filmmakers and writers to fuel that with their creative endeavors! Some efforts will undoubtedly be more enjoyable and better crafted than others, which is true of any legitimate art form or artistic expression. It would be interesting to see what kind of movie could be made about Pythian Castle with an acting cast to match!

The Phantom of Valley Water Mill

The Valley Water Mill and its dam is an interesting place to visit and, cut off from the flow of most traffic, it bears closer examination for haunting activity. Driving on North Glenstone (Highway H), turn right onto Farm Road 94E, and turn right again onto East Valley Water Mill Road.

I have often heard the story of a phantom horseman riding in this area, but I've never seen it personally. Legend says it is a tall, bearded man wearing a Confederate military dress with cape and feathered Southern hat; he is riding a black horse. His saber is drawn, and he appears to be looking for either a person or an object. He is intense, talking and pointing with his saber to the ground, perhaps indicating the burial site of something valuable not to fall in the hands of the Union soldiers. By his bearing, he is seen as an officer. His gray, uniformed image lingers briefly...and then vanishes.

Valley Water Mill is now in the planning stage for a wetlands ecosystem. Strange stories have been passed down over the years about this area. There are three caves on the land, one discovered and two still hidden.

Walking this land in April 2008 gave me the feeling that there was something waiting here...*something waiting to happen*. What it is, I have no idea.

Highway 13

This highway has an uneasy feel about it at different places. The stretch of highway from Bolivar, Missouri down to Springfield, Missouri seems to contain a genuine atmosphere of haunting about it. There have been many accidents on the highway.

This highway also connects to the Kansas City, Missouri area. There is a record of vehicle accidents in this area, too.

I found driving it by car put me in a tense mood only in the last five miles outside Springfield leading into the city...as if there was some strange situation being waged or fought in that area. It gave me a feeling of unease. I have had that feeling several times driving this route, as has my wife, Debra, when she is with me in the car. *There is some situation or some* **THING** *there, very real...but not visible to the naked eye.*

The Bobbing Heads of James River

James River has its share of hauntings, many of them related to known, forgotten, or unknown drownings. Located in Southern Missouri, it has its original water source near Diggins, Missouri in Webster County.

James River passes near Springfield and flows to Galena, connecting with Table Rock Lake and becoming a tributary of White River. Over the decades, there have been reports of swimmers in this river who simply appear, swim a short distance, dive, and then vanish. Some bobbing heads have been seen on the surface of this river, and then sink away beneath the water. There have been many drownings in the James River.

Are these the remnants of children whose bodies were never found, or bodies of dead American Civil War soldiers left to sink and become part of the river, or settlers, or American Indians who lived in the area? Different faces have been seen. Children, women, and men belong to those nameless faces. These bobbing heads are now lost in time, *RESIDUAL HAUNTINGS* of some other place, situation, scene, and time.

There is a large volume of writings about ghosts from drownings, and the theme has been used in movies and fiction over the decades. Where there is a drowning, there is generally the possibility of a ghost connected with it in some manner, but not always.

Phelps Grove Park

950 East Bennett Street

Phelps Grove has thirty-one acres, which includes a xeriscape garden and a long stone pavilion building. The restrooms are considered haunted in the pavilion and laughter has been heard there.

The laughter is not loud and can be either male or female. No sign of bodies, just ghost voices. Shadow figures have been seen in the stone pavilion building.

Phelps Grove Park.

The Ghost of Bud Isbell

The ghost of a young black man, identified as Bud Isbell, is an interesting look at early social and racial history in Springfield. In June 1871, Bud Isbell went to the home of Peter A. Christian and raped his white wife.

Captured, Isbell was brought back to Springfield to be tried for his crime of rape. A man named Major R. B. Chappel advised the crowd to be sure of his guilt for the crime of raping a white woman before punishment was doled out to this twenty-one year old accused male.

There was no trial...just a lynching. The hanging was botched, but carried through. To make sure Bud Isbell was dead he was shot by three different men. His dead body was abused and he was castrated.

Later, after the hanging, a formal jury found the dead man guilty as accused, and stated his death was caused by hanging and gunshots. According to reports at the time, Bud Isbell had also raped a young colored girl.

Thus, in the words of the time, that was the way of it. Bud Isbell's big, lumbering ghost was said to haunt the Springfield City area until after the start of World War I, when he ceased to frighten people by materializing before them and suddenly vanishing with an evil grin on his rough features.

The Ghost of Martin Danforth

In mid-August 1859, Martin Danforth, a black man, raped the white wife of John Morrow of Springfield. He was identified by the woman as the rapist and taken into custody and questioned. Martin Danforth, also known as Mart Danforth, confessed to the crime.

Before he could be arraigned for trial, Danforth was taken from his confinement room in the Springfield Public Square area. A lynching was to be his fate rather than a trial.

At this point in time, slaves or estate Negroes were generally castrated in such a crude manner as to ensure that no such offense would take place ever again. Martin Danforth was hanged immediately and then castrated.

In another episode involving rape of a white woman by a black man, Bud Isbell (see previous story) was hanged near the same spot as Martin Danforth. The ghost of a moaning Martin Danforth haunted his hanging tree for a short time and then never returned.

Springfield Landfill

The Springfield Landfill is found by taking Highway 13 from Springfield towards Morrisville. Access is by turning left onto a paved road off of the highway. The area has its own set of "sounds," which include voices and laughter. Nothing is ever seen, only the sounds. The wind has an odd sound about it at the landfill location, sometimes a whisper and other times a banshee cry.

It's my belief that all things contain some touch of past contact. I have had this proven to me again and again over the years.

I believe a trash dump, a forgotten dumpsite, or even an active landfill area can hold clues to the past. Be they ever so minor or small, each article trashed has gone through existence and retained a psychic impression on its surface or interior. This may explain in part why more psychics are becoming involved in archaeological onsite investigations. What may have been lost in time to the individual untrained in such matters may be reclaimable by the accurate approach of psychics skilled and trained in examining artifacts by touch with their bodies and minds.

There are books available that will train an individual in the different methods of discovering the past history of an object. For instance, an individual, who can read the past of an artifact, may come across a large weathered bank key or jail key. Upon concentration and reflection, images should appear suggesting what the key did in its lifetime. The images are written down, and further documentation is undertaken to confirm, verify, or ascertain the background of such images — when did they exist, who was involved, what happened.

Don't overlook the possibilities of dumpsites. Those that have been abandoned for decades may hold the greatest prizes of all, depending upon what you are seeking. It's always important to recall the fact that artifacts can have ghosts or haunting situations connected with them. Some of these unusual items find themselves up for sale in different settings.

Take a look at the listings for haunted rings and haunted keys available for bid on eBay — you'd be surprised with the variety and availability for sale. You will find some items that claim to have a spell or incantation placed upon them, or others that claim to come from some haunted or historical settings. The possibilities are fascinating and interesting to investigate.

Despite the ongoing efforts of Hollywood movies, not all hauntings are bad. Not all ghosts are bad.

The scene of a haunting, the object or item of a haunting, and the presence of paranormal activity involving ghosts oftentimes occur to offer a clue to an event that took place in the past. They may also be there to offer instruction of some type. Remember: *Paranormal activity is a form of existential reality based on pre-existing sequences in time.*

Haunted Old Railroad Yard and Tracks

The original railroad yard, tracks, and depot structures of Springfield have long since undergone massive changes and repairs, but their long and colorful history includes paranormal activity. Sightings of railroad accident victims and reputed contact with the spirits of those who died in this railroad area under uncommon or unsolved circumstances are not unusual. There are frequent hauntings at railroad tracks or locations associated with train traffic throughout the United States.

I walked in what is called the Yard, and it was interesting to sense the many presences in this lively area of past history. Walking the area gives one a sense of the past blending with the present. I came across a heavy-set older man wearing a coverall outfit and bill cap. I waved at him, the

Railroad Yards.

distance between us about twenty feet. He was carrying one of those old-fashioned lunch pails.

"You lookin' for something, Mister?" he asked.

"No, nothing in particular. I'm writing about the paranormal in Missouri, thought I'd check this area out," I replied.

"What's paranormal?"

"Ghosts," I answered.

"Ghosts?" he said, and there came a loud, solid laugh with that response. "Well, you come to the right place. There's ghosts in this place, all over the place! There's bodies buried here, too. The west area and south area has some buried bodies nobody knows are there! Ghosts! You tell 'em Roland said there are ghosts and bodies here."

"I will," I said. "Thanks!"

He turned abruptly and went on his way, walking slowly alongside the tracks, a slight limp to his left leg. I went on my way. I walked a short distance, turned, and looked back towards the open expanse of railroad tracks. **ROLAND WAS GONE**. The area was clear and visible. There were no obstructions to my view, but Roland was not there.

I would suggest there are other ghosts here. *The old railroad yard and tracks are a paranormal shelter for both intelligent and residual hauntings.* I wonder what era the ghost of Roland is from and why he still haunts this railroad area.

Is Roland a ghost watchman looking out for the dead? Is he a ghost who does not know he is dead? Or is he a victim not yet at rest?

The Bluegrass Farm

The Bluegrass Farm is what my Uncle Les and Aunt Margaret called their home on RFD 10 in Greene County, not far from the city of Springfield. In 2008, that old Bluegrass Road would be identified as Farm Road 94. Aunt Margaret was my Grandmother Archie Tennessee (Blythe) Firestone's sister, which made her my great aunt, and Uncle Les my great uncle. Uncle Les and Aunt Margaret were a devoted, loving couple, and they were the greatest relatives a child could have anywhere or anyplace!

Les and Margaret Caudle were an interesting couple. They owned a large, two hundred plus acreage past the Valley Water Mill area that was home to much livestock. It was a second home to me growing up as a child, as I spent much time there until Uncle Les' death, the selling of the property, and Aunt Margaret relocating to live with her son, Everett, and his wife and three daughters in Texas. Aunt Margaret would die in Texas of old age.

I greatly admired Uncle Les' approach to rural living, and as a retired Frisco Railroad employee, he always had some remarkable story to share with me. I also remember sleeping at their comfortable country farmhouse on a bed with two feather mattresses, one to sleep under and one to cover up with. What a treat that was for a kid growing up, kind of like being in a cushioned, floating bed!

I recall Uncle Les taking me to a cave on the property that had served as a refuge spot for traveling American Indians. He had found evidence of the Indians' stay there, including arrowheads, spearheads, pottery, and some discarded artwork on rock pieces. The problem was his cows and pigs would get inside the cave and then were difficult to get out. It was not a large cave, but it did extend some distance; how far or how deep I do not remember.

Friends of his in the construction business dynamited the cave entrance and successfully collapsed it to spare any further problems with the livestock. The Indian artifacts were left intact and are still there as far as I know. When the work was completed, a casual passerby would not have guessed a cave was hidden there.

There was a creek with some good deep spots, and this is where I saw my first shadow figures as a child. I also learned to swim there, too, for my Uncle Willard carefully, and with much gentleness, surprised me by dumping me into the water from the bank, and laughing, shouted, "Swim, Lee, swim!" Uncle Willard hit the water at few seconds behind me to make sure I wasn't in any danger. I sputtered around for a few seconds, flapped my hands, remembered what Uncle Willard had shown me about swim strokes, and I did swim! From that point on, it was next to impossible to keep me from swimming. I recall seeing water moccasin snakes, but I also recall Uncle Willard saying to stand perfectly still if they passed you on the water surface or under water, and they would leave you alone. I did, and they left me alone.

One afternoon, I saw an elderly woman walking on the bank while I was swimming — she walked right into thin air and vanished. Searching my memory, my guess was she was an early settler in that part of Missouri, possibly on her way to get water. I can still recall her blue gingham dress and white bonnet. As I was not noticed or approached, I'd classify this as a residual haunting.

I told Uncle Les about the experience, and he smiled, saying, "You see a lot more in the country sometimes than you bargain for, Lee." Later, when I went back to Springfield, I told Uncle Willard about what I had seen and what Uncle Les had told me. He agreed.

I'd like to clarify some background here, and that is, Uncle Willard was the closest person to a father I had growing up in my formative years and he did well by me in that role. In Springfield, I lived with my Uncle Willard, my mother, Marjorie, and my Grandmother Firestone. My childhood was normal in the sense I had friends and went different places. It was an enjoyable home life as I remember it. But it was more than normal in the sense that my Uncle Willard was both father image and mentor to me, all in one package! As a father image, he filled that role to perfection, and it was only as a young adult that I learned my (real) father had deserted me after World War II, divorced my mother, and remarried to start a second family. It was not until I was an adult that I did make peace with my father, Harold, and we came to know each other in a somewhat limited but genuine manner as blood kin.

As a student learning from Uncle Willard, I soaked up knowledge like a sponge and came to understand about the supernatural, the occult, the paranormal, different religions, and different secret societies. I thrived on it, learned, and absorbed everything I could. Uncle Willard seemed to know just the right moment to introduce some new concept or idea, which took hold in my mind and allowed me to explore it.

Whereas my mother was either working, dating, or going bowling most of the time and Grandmother Firestone was involved in her Eastern Star activities and Baptist Church gatherings, Uncle Willard was my constant companion and taught me many things, and in the purest sense of the statement, Uncle Willard made me what I am, guiding me to become what I was to become as a man. That is why I am a Vedantist, a lifelong researcher of the occult, and Master of the Temple in the Order of the Golden Dawn.

Interestingly enough, Uncle Willard set me up on my first date with a female and told me how to behave, what to expect, and what not to say. Yes, I learned a lot from Willard David Firestone! Another insight he shared with me, which I did not fully understand until I was older and more seasoned, was that sometimes you have to stand up against the pressures of family and friends if you intuitively know your way is the right way for you if not for them. A decent, kind man, Uncle Willard never hurt any person or animal in his life, and lived his values and beliefs instead of merely talking about them. He walked the walk he talked and did not ever vary, but was always honest in his intent. He was employed as a master dental technician for over fifty years and decades of exposure to the acrylic dust used to make the dentures eventually gave him the liver cancer that he died from.

Although as a philosophical approach, which I read, understood, and observed throughout my lifetime, it was Uncle Willard who best personified for me the old existential theme of endurance: First of all you endure. Then, anything else is secondary. Your actions define what you become. Yes, I would willingly say without any bias that was the epitome of Uncle Willard as a man.

Willard was also a keen observer of human nature and a listener, not a talker. He always believed that actions were more important than words. I agree with him because I have found it's true. As a child growing into manhood, I then formulated my personal code in the following manner: *Intent is everything and anything else is secondary to intent.*

I recall another time at Uncle Les' rural home when I saw the ghost of a timber wolf and thought the damn thing was going to eat me alive! What big teeth that monster had in its mouth! But it didn't eat me...it simply passed on its way, unaware of my presence. It vanished as quickly as it had arrived in my world and went on its way hunting in its paranormal world. Another time, when I was probably around eleven years old, I was swimming in the creek and saw an American Indian looking down on me from the bank above. I am not sure to this day whether he was attempting an intelligent contact, which would have made this an intelligent haunting, or quietly fascinated by something near me in the water. Whatever his motive or paranormal goal, his eyes followed my movements in the water without pause and I think he wanted to make contact. I said hello several times, but that had no reaction on him, nor did he show any recognition of my speaking to him. At some point in his watchfulness, he blinked his eyelids, turned, and slowly walked away. I climbed out of the water and reached the bank...only to see nothing there. No sign of this man, nothing.

About this same time, in late summer, I saw several military men riding horses along the creek bank. These ten men rode in formation. I was old enough to have seen the outfits the Confederates and the Union soldiers wore during the war and these were Union soldiers. I would say they were probably out on a patrol or on a mission. I yelled "Hi!" at them in a loud voice several times, but they went right on their way, passing along, talking to each other, totally oblivious to a young boy in the water.

There were many such incidents like these, each different, when I visited the rural home of my Uncle Les and Aunt Margaret. Their home is long since demolished; it had been built on the grounds of their first home, which had burned down.

Their first house had been filled with antiques, old glassware, and rare coins. As an enterprising business my Aunt Margaret had going for herself, she collected and sold such items to friends and customers interested in antique artifacts from the past. The original fire destroyed everything, but there was always plenty of items to be found slightly below the surface or scattered about loosely in the soil within a four hundred foot circumference of where they rebuilt their new home. I don't know how many porcelain doll heads, doll parts, coins, and pieces of glassware I discovered on my frequent trips to visit Uncle Les and Aunt Margaret. There was always something of interest to do there, and like most enterprising children, I found plenty of things to get into!

College Hauntings

There are three higher education institutions in Springfield that have hauntings and ghosts due to incidents that occurred at their locations or related to the land on which they were established. They are Evangel, Drury, and Missouri State Universities.

In 1955, the Assemblies of God Church established a Pentecostal liberal arts college named Evangel College at 1111 North Glenstone Avenue. It is now situated on eighty acres, but it wasn't always a college that sat on this land! O'Reilly General Army Hospital was established on the land originally in 1941, and its Post Commander was Colonel George B. Foster, Jr. During World War II, this hospital setting took care of over 100,000 patients and had a civilian staff of over 1,000. This Army hospital was the pride of the United States Army Medical Corps and was the standard by which all others were judged. During the war, and through 1945, there were many celebrities who visited and entertained the soldiers at this hospital, including pianist Jose Iturbi and actresses Gloria Stuart and Hillary Brook. Gloria Stuart is a prolific actress, her film career getting underway in the early 1930s with such movies as "The Old Dark House" (1932) starring Boris Karloff, "The Three Musketeers" (1939) and more recently, the role of the old woman in "Land of Plenty" (2004). Her most memorable film role is that of the old woman in the blockbuster movie, "Titanic" (1997). Hillary Brooke (1914–1999) made many television series appearances and her film career started in the 1930s. Among Hillary Brooke's films were two popular films from 1946, the film noir classic "The Strange Woman" and "Strange Journey."

There was suffering and people did die of their war wounds, but overall O'Reilly was a hospital that tended to its wounded soldiers with great caring, skill, and kindness. As a hospital, if the word "happy" can be used, it was a happy place and the medical personnel and civilian staff made it so with their positive attitudes.

Evangel University clock tower.

There were haunting stories told of the hospital: ghost soldiers were known to walk the corridors; the sounds of different male voices singing 1940s popular songs such as "You Always Hurt The One You Love," "Be Careful, It's My Heart," "I'll Be Seeing You," and "You'd Be So Nice To Come Home To," were heard; shadow figures prowled the numerous buildings; and ghosts were seen in different buildings. Yes, a gaggle of ghost stories about this hospital were popular at one time.

Now, with little to recall its full heritage as a wartime hospital, this land is the site for a well-known and respected church education center of higher learning. It would be interesting to study this modern day campus and see if there are still as many active shadow figures, hauntings, ghostly voices and spectors. Or has the passage of time dimmed such happenings into oblivion by being ignored? Is there some active touch of them still there? One can't help but wonder. An elderly man told me the ground on which the Evangel Library was built is extremely haunted.

Drury University is another haunted location, given its unique history. Located at 900 North Benton, Drury is blessed with a charming appearance, but its old buildings have an impressive enchantment of their own. Established in 1873 by Congregationalists, it eventually spread out and grew into a well-respected ninety-acre campus. With its emphasis on positive values and the work ethic, it has survived different hardships brought on by such economic problems as the Great Depression of the 1930s. As a private higher education setting, it has endured well over the decades.

Pearson Hall was opened in 1902 and is still in use today. McCullagh Hall opened as a girls' dormitory in 1884 and served as barracks during World War II; it was demolished in 1969. Stone Chapel, with its Victorian-Gothic appearance, is one of the magnificent stone structures still standing and in use. Of the various academic buildings, the Stone Chapel and the President's House are reputed to have some type of haunting. Stone Chapel has orbs and shadow figures. It depends on whom you ask about this setting as to what types of hauntings have taken place. Some of these hauntings involve seeing ghosts that appear one minute and vanish the next. Walking this campus on Benton Avenue during the early evening hours is like taking a pleasant stroll into a more endearing historical time when people were more inclined to taking life quietly and appreciated social values. I could sense ghost presences around me as I walked the campus and investigated the Stone Chapel. They seemed as curious about me as I was about them.

Drury University is across from Central High School. The attics and basements at Drury have long been reputed to have hauntings. Numerous stories told through the decades and recent encounters could be a combination of both intelligent and residual hauntings taking

Stone Chapel, Drury University.

Missouri State University haunted building.

place. Although I did not visit the attics or basements, I did investigate the campus, walking around it and sensing what might be about. I did encounter ghosts of a residual haunting there.

Missouri State University, known affectionately in the community as MSU, is a state teacher's college originally established at the turn of the century in 1905. Located at 901 South National Avenue, it's a lively educational setting with a large, diverse student body. It has various degree programs available.

I got my second degree from there. I earned a Bachelor of Science in Sociology in 1974. The campus and the surrounding neighborhoods have greatly changed since that time. Places I ate breakfast at, areas I walked, or places I visited no longer exist. Much has been demolished, with the land now being used for other purposes.

The older buildings on campus have residual hauntings. Some of the upper floors seem to attract positive presences, and if you reach out to feel for their presences, you will find them. I recall seeing the ghost of a redheaded woman dressed in 1940s clothing in the library once; she appeared, walked a short distance, and disappeared around a corner inside the building. I thought she went into what was then the typing room, but on examination, she had vanished at the door. The typing room was empty at the time.

The campus has a long and colorful history, and today, occupies 220 acres in central Springfield. MSU also has an impressive list of people who attended or graduated from its campus, including actor John Goodman, actresses Tess Harper and Kathleen Turner, and many sports and business figures of importance.

Part One: Spirits in Springfield, Missouri

Missouri State University haunted building, number two.

Carrington Hall, built in 1908, is one of its most haunted buildings. Depending on whom you visit with, you are bound to come across many stories of various types of hauntings, ghosts, and orbs on the Missouri State University campus.

Springfield National Cemetery

1702 East Seminole Street

This large cemetery is primarily for veterans of wars, is approximately eighteen acres in size, and was established in 1867 not long after the

Springfield National Cemetery, Confederate Pavilion.

Placard legend on pavilion wall.

American Civil War memorial statue.

conclusion of the American Civil War. It's located at 1702 East Seminole and became listed on the Register of Historical Places in 1999. With monuments and memorials to see, this is an interesting war dead cemetery to visit.

Orbs have been seen at twilight in the cemetery. Residual hauntings with Union and Confederate soldiers have also been seen.

I became aware of a Confederate soldier at the center of the cemetery, but could get no set image of him. A Union soldier was walking towards me in the west section, but vanished within fifteen feet of where I was standing. A World War II Navy man in full dress with cap was running down the south section…only to vanish near a monument. I would say this cemetery has its fair share of residual hauntings for those interested and attuned to these ghostly presences.

City Hall

Opened in 1894, this building served as the original post office and customs clearing location for the county. Located at the corner of Boonville

Springfield City Hall gargoyle.

Springfield City Hall.

Avenue and Chestnut Expressway, it's an imposing building with an unusual architectural design. It's noted for its stone turrets and gargoyle waterspouts. The south wing has a tower.

There are four ghost stories associated with this old building. The second floor is reputed to have an elderly lady ghost, and the third floor is said to have the ghosts of a newspaperman and a judge. The tower on the south wing is believed to have the ghost of a smiling janitor with broom in hand.

Ghostly phenomena aside, if you're in the area, the gargoyles are splendid works of art and well worth your time to photograph them.

Public Library

Located at the corner of Central Avenue and Jefferson Street, this large building has two stories and a basement. It opened to the public in 1905. Three ghost stories have come to be attached to this building over the decades.

One is that the ghost of a young boy haunts the basement area and is said to laugh. The second story involves a cold spot in the men's restroom and the sounds of labored breathing. The third ghost story is of an elderly

Public Library.

man who has been seen in the reading room ... he vanishes upon approach by the living!

I spent much time in this library as a youngster, either checking out books or researching topics of interest. I never saw the ghost of the young boy, but I sensed several presences in the reading room on different occasions. I also could feel the cold spot in the men's bathroom.

Other Springfield Sightings

Barth's Clothing Store

This old brick building with many windows was built in 1838 and has had several different owners. Located at 154 Park Central Square, it's a historic building site.

Orbs have been seen inside the structure, through the windows, at night. The ghost of a young boy in a Boy Scout uniform is reputed to haunt the second floor.

Grant Beach Park

Grant Beach Park is located at 833 West Calhoun Street. On its fifteen acres is located a fenced train exhibit. This artifact is the restored Frisco Locomotive number 4524 with commuter car and caboose attached to it.

I swam here as a child in the 1950s. The Frisco Locomotive has always had a reputation of having shadow figures about it at different times.

Shady Inn

Located near Sunshine and Campbell Streets, Shady Inn was a popular drinking and eating establishment for decades. It opened in 1947 and was noted for its fine steak dinners. It was reputed to have a ghost chef who appeared after the place closed for the night. It has since been demolished, with nothing remaining of its passing.

In 2008, I was given personal gifts of the decorative glass block sections from the back bar of the restaurant. These glass sections contain haunted images from the life and times of this famous restaurant. The psychic images within the glass are interesting to study and view—as both my wife Debra and I have discovered!

The Grove

Located on Glenstone Road, not far from Division, The Grove had a large following as an interesting place to gather, drink, and visit. It opened in 1947 and had some class acts that came there, such as singers. It was reputed to have a male ghost trumpet player who appeared after closing hours and would play a lonely blues song. Like Shady Inn, The Grove was demolished.

St. John's Hospital

The original hospital site is said to be built on land once occupied by American Indians during the very early part of the nineteenth century. At the same time, another settlement with a different tribe was located due west.

The St. John Hospital system had its origins with the founder, Catherine McAuley, in Dublin, Ireland, and became part of the Catholic order of nuns named Sisters of Mercy. Located at 1235 East Cherokee, it was first established as a twenty-bed hospital in 1891.

The older sections of the hospital have had hauntings, mostly residual and short-lived. There are shadow figures seen, and there has been laughter heard in the halls. This hospital has been a long and useful medical setting for the city, and continues to develop as a large medical facility in recent years.

Ritter Springs Park

Ritter Springs Park is located at 3683 West Farm Road 92. It contains 246 acres and a lake. Ten to fifteen Union soldiers in the process of burying weapons are said to haunt the park.

Another ghost story is that the area contains the bodies of buried Union soldiers who were not given a Christian burial at the time of internment and forever walk the grounds in sadness. Voices without bodies have been heard near the lake, and during the summer months, mists appear and dissolve into shadow figures.

River Bluff Cave

Located at 2327 West Farm Road 190, River Bluff Cave House has thirty-four acres and a cave. Shadow figures have been seen near the cave area. The cave is closed to the public.

Sequiota Park

Sequiota Park is located at 3500 South Lone Pine Street. It's a twenty-eight acre park with a cave and a lake. There is a story of a young woman who was found dead in the park in the 1940s; it's now believed that she haunts the lake and cave.

Another story is of a young boy who drowned in the lake and haunts the lake during the night hours. Orbs have been seen over the lake and near the cave. There are several ghost stories about this park involving the lake and cave, but these are the two most prevalent. An animal haunting involving a white cat near the cave is another story.

The Streets of Springfield

For many different reasons, certain houses or locations seem conducive to hauntings and the supernatural. There may be a house on a street that has some record of activity, or perhaps an empty parcel of land, or tree, or a sidewalk. Ghosts can and do select an area, and whether it's an intelligent or a residual haunting, it does take place. It does happen!

Too often, an individual will dismiss that certain prickling at the back of the neck as a breeze, but it's a good sign that something paranormal is happening or about to happen. To be open and perceptive to one's immediate surroundings allows one to glimpse the other side.

We are never alone. There is more to those planes of paranormal existence than mere human flesh and bone is aware of. If you want to know and experience paranormal situations, you have to be ready to commit to opening yourself to them. You have to allow what wants to show itself to you to do exactly that.

Here are some streets you may wish to walk at your convenience: Jefferson, St. Louis, Walnut, Elm, National, Grand, Olive, Water, East, Blaine, Sunset, Locust, Summit, Washington, Catalina, Clay, Kimbrough, Dale, Atlantic, Benton, Pacific, Grant, and Central.

The Smiling Black Priest

A Catholic priest has been seen near the corner of Elm Street and South Jefferson Avenue. He is walking quickly and turns the corner at Elm and Jefferson going south—and then vanishes.

The priest is a young, slender black man and he's smiling. What was his mission? Where is he going with such determined steps?

Zagonyi Park

Zagonyi Park is located at Mt. Vernon Street and Park Avenue. It has ten acres. Shadow figures have been seen here. The laughter of an invisible woman can also be heard.

U.S. Medical Center for Federal Prisoners

The United States Medical Center for Federal Prisoners is located at 1900 West Sunshine Street and has approximately 257 acres under its direct jurisdiction. Prisoner riots occurred there in the 1940s, with its last riot in 1959.

Opened in 1933, it houses over 1,000 prisoners. Among the famous prisoners incarcerated there were Robert Stroud and John Gotti. American Indian activist Leonard Peltier is still alive and incarcerated there.

Over the decades there have been horror stories told concerning brutality among the prisoner population. There have been many reputed stories of paranormal occurrences including hauntings.

2

Something's Amiss in Aurora, Missouri

Aurora, Missouri is located in Lawrence County and has some strange hauntings, many of them extremely macabre and scary. The county was organized in 1845 and has a long history as a lead and zinc mining location. Although not large numbers of soldiers were killed, during the American Civil War skirmishes between the North and the South did take place frequently.

Underwater Demons in the Mines

Mining opened in 1873 in and around Aurora, and continued until 1955. Abandoned, these underground mines filled rapidly with uncontrolled ground water. Later designated as the Lawrence County Mining Sites, there were two large mining areas in and around the city of Aurora. Part of Baldwin Park, which has a history of lead and zinc mining on the property, was at one time used for public dumping.

Underwater divers have investigated some of the mines. There was an incident where divers returned to the surface frightened and now nobody is allowed to dive that mine section. Stories of underwater demons and ghosts lurking in the mines are commonplace, and different versions have been talked about. There are accounts of wrecked automobiles and trucks in the mines — and of bodies still in them. An account of a bright, white skeleton floating through a broken automobile window after a diver is told around campfires.

Beware of the soft female voice calling **YOUR** name... She appears to be behind you, but is never seen.

Or a woman's laugh... the laughing woman is said to laugh three separate times. But again, she's **NEVER** seen—only her loud laugh is heard.

The entrance to one forgotten mine is said to be guarded by the ghost of a very attractive redheaded woman in her early twenties. She

Old vintage postcard of the Aurora mines.

stands naked, beckoning to all who come her way. She is tall, lean, and long-legged. Her outstretched arms beckon to those who have seen her comely body with its full white breasts and hard red nipples. There is a sense of wantonness in her lovely square-jawed face. She is seen either with blue eyes or with dark, seemingly empty eye sockets. She is smiling a look of pleasure for all to see, but her full lips never move from her fixed smile...this ghost woman does not speak. She may be a murder victim entombed in the mines, seeking revenge with a time-tested approach she hopes will lure a victim to her watery grave to lie beside her.

Stories of heads without bodies shimmering near the mine floors have been part of the ghost lore. Shadowy creatures without form haunt the underwater mines freely and do not like visitors from the human world above. Shadow figures have also been seen on the surface near former mine entrances or over a stretch of mines that lies deep below. Strange mutations that are part human and part something else lurk in the mine depths and on occasion walk the land near the mines.

Old Mine Number 59 is among the mines to be avoided if you value your life, is another story told, because of underwater demons lurking about the mine walls. These mines are full of hauntings, below and aboveground.

In 2008, there was discussion among government officials about arranging for the burial of many of these mines. The plan is to dig down twenty feet or more into the entrance of each mine, place a concrete and rock plug into each mine's exposed opening, and then dynamite the wall sides to create an avalanche of dirt, sealing up each mine forever.

How the ghostly inhabitants within those mines will take such action poses an interesting dilemma! Only time will tell if the hauntings continue.

Princess Theater

14 West Olive Street

Built in 1943, this comfortable theater with a unique interior has been a family favorite in the Aurora area since the time of World War II. It's located at 14 West Olive Street.

There have been sightings of two World War II American sailors in dress uniforms walking down the street towards the theater entrance. They vanish before reaching it. Another version, or perhaps a different haunting, is of an American sailor in dress uniform and a young woman wearing 1940s era clothes holding hands and silently laughing together. The young couple is walking down the street towards the theater entrance and…they, too, vanish before reaching it. Not often seen now, this is an example of a residual haunting.

Shadow figures have also been seen inside the theater.

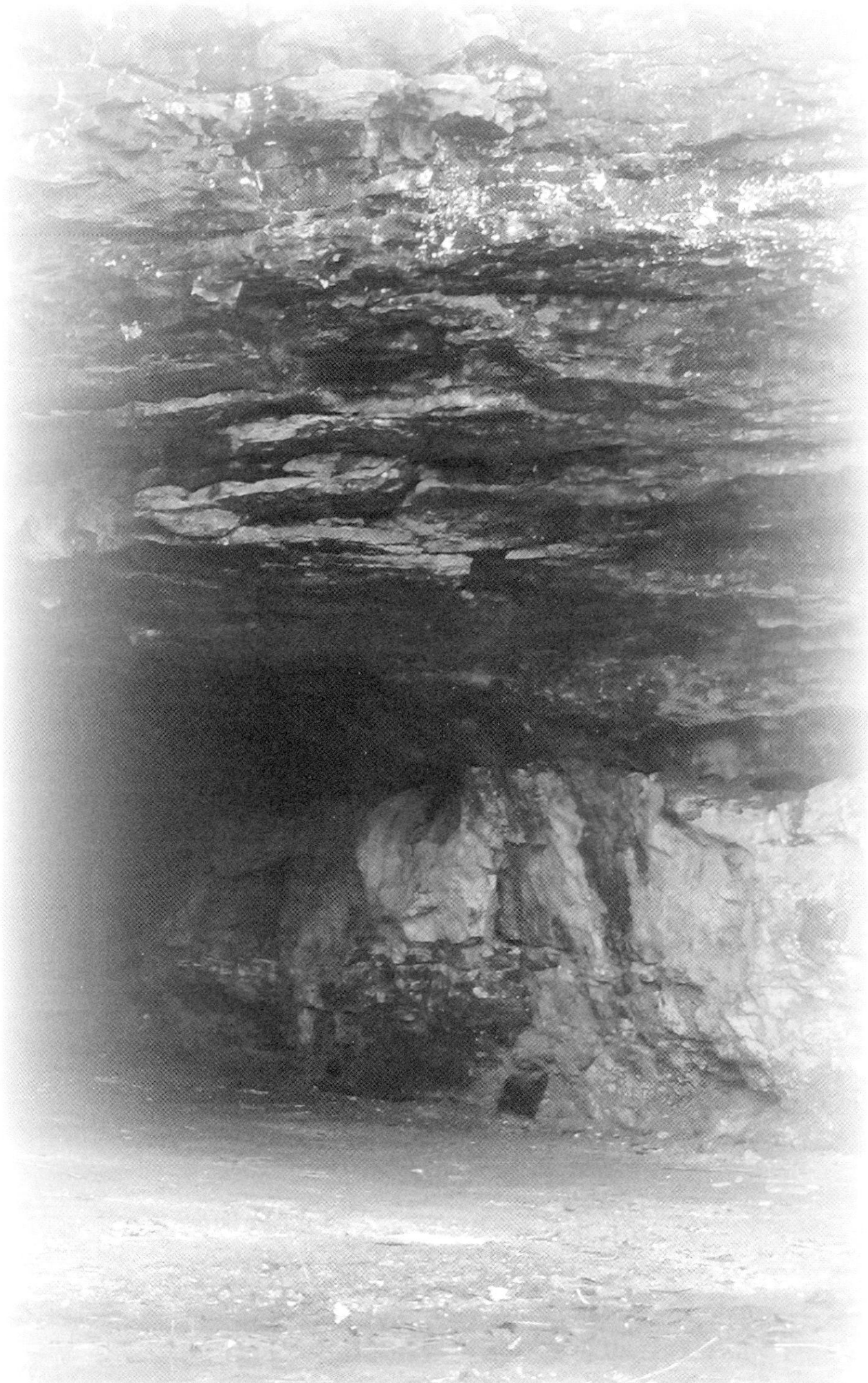

3

Barely There in Branson, Missouri

Branson, Missouri has become known worldwide as the Live Music Capital of the World, becoming one of the most popular places to visit. Its villains and outlaws include the Bald Knobbers, Frank and Jesse James, the Younger Brothers, Bonnie & Clyde, and Alf Bolin. That the American Civil War made Missouri lawless is a fact.

Rueben Branson opened a general store and post office in 1882, and homesteaders moved into the colorful, beautiful area not long after. In 1894 William Henry Lynch purchased a cave outside of Branson, and this cave would one day become the world-famous Marvel Cave. Marvel Cave is located six miles outside of Branson.

In 1907 the novel, *The Shepherd of the Hills*, by Harold Bell Wright was published, making the Branson area and the Missouri Ozarks a popular place to visit. The book became a huge national bestseller, and further spread the word about the Missouri Ozarks. People came from everywhere to see the area.

The Hauntings...

On April 1, 1912, Branson became incorporated and the emphasis was on tourism. Table Rock Dam and Table Rock Lake were completed in 1963. Since that time, Branson has become an entertainment and retirement center for Missouri. Among the many entertainers having their own theaters and performing in Branson are Shoji Tabuchi, Mel Tillis, Andy Williams, Bobby Vinton, and Christy Lane.

There are numerous ghost stories surrounding the Branson area and Marvel Cave. Many unnerving things have been seen.

The ghost of Frank James has been seen near Marvel Cave. The ghost of Jesse James has been seen near the outskirts of old downtown Branson.

Talking Rocks Cavern, Powell Cave, and Mud Cave have regular visits from shadow figures. A ghost horse was seen at Talking Rocks Cavern.

Old vintage postcard of Branson, Missouri.

A young, wounded Confederate soldier was seen at the riverbank clutching his private area and bleeding profusely — a war wound or victim of castration by the Union forces? Did he bleed to death there and his body later claimed by nature? As a commentary, it's fair to say that sexual mutilation goes hand-in-hand with civilization and is not limited to any one country. It's a time-honored practice against one's enemy, but remains a dishonored deed against humanity—and it produces its share of hauntings. A practice older than the Ancient Greeks and Ancient Romans, the belief is that if you mutilate your victim in some way that affects the reproductive organs, that person will be rendered impotent, unable to reproduce, and will be denied his or her missing parts in the afterlife. It's a shameful act done to render the victims worthless in their own eyes, as they are forced to watch their own mutilation. Dead bodies were also hacked-up, sliced, and mutilated.

There are horror stories about Southern women mutilating the black female slaves who were lovers of their husbands during the American Civil War. Castration was a penalty often used by slaveholders against their slaves. There are stories of sexual mutilation by both the Union and the Confederacy in the American Civil War. Sexual mutilations during the French Revolution were also not uncommon. Various women warriors throughout history carried out castration and mutilation against victims, as such treatment was done to both males and females.

The settling of the American Wild West is full of such atrocities. There are also the horror stories of mutilation carried out by Union soldiers against American Indian men, women, and children; an examination of the massacre at Wounded Knee is a prime example.

At Wounded Knee, Union soldiers castrated their victims for the pleasure of having a scrotum sack for a tobacco pouch, or slicing off a woman's breasts for the same purpose. Many of these victims were still alive and died after the heinous act.

Cutting off a woman's labia was another torture, with the dried, preserved pieces of the labia given away to friends as gifts. As a good luck token or totem, it was akin to carrying around a lucky rabbit's foot. Oftentimes, a male's penis was sliced off at the base, and the member preserved with liquid in a glass jar as a souvenir. There are stories of such containers being found in basements of abandoned old homes across the United States.

There is much documentation on these practices available over the centuries in various books and other records. World War I and World War II are full of such acts, as was the Vietnam War.

When the Nazi Germany concentration camps of World War II were opened up, it was revealed that the private parts of both men and women were used to make lampshades, wallets, purses, bookbindings, and other items. Different concentration camps had different approaches, different techniques, and freely performed various medical experiments on the prisoners.

Practices of sexual mutilations are widespread today in Islamic countries. The late dictator Saddam Hussein of Iraq was noted for ordering or personally performing sexual mutilations against his many enemies.

Just because these things do not always make the news does not mean they are not happening on a daily basis. You need only look at what is happening in today's headlines to know such actions continue unabated.

Sexual mutilation is the supreme act of physical abuse that can be carried out on a victim. How many ghosts may be suffering shock and death as a result of such a wounding? Humankind is the only species that tortures for pleasure. It's something to consider when investigating haunted locations by asking, were such acts carried out on this person or at that location? History is interpreted by its victors, but the truth will eventually make its way to the surface no matter how deeply it's buried with its victims.

Back to the hauntings, there are stories of shadow figures along roadsides and highways in and around Branson. *The Shepherd of the Hills* historic site contains ghost sightings. A woman singing in a clear voice the words of the song, "The Old Rugged Cross," has been heard near Old Matt's cabin. The cabin is haunted and voices have been heard around it and inside it with nobody ever being present.

The ghosts of Country Western singers Conway Twitty (1933–1993), Waylon Jennings (1937–2002), Hank Williams, Sr. (1923–1953), Marty Robbins (1925–1982), and Freddy Fender (1937–2006) have been seen in different music theaters.

Part Three: Barely There in Branson, Missouri

Old vintage postcard of Old Matt's Cabin.

There have been sightings of American Civil War soldiers riding horses in the woods of Branson, and walking pioneer settlers dressed in the clothing of their time. Ghost horses that run and vanish have been seen.

As this lively town continues to grow, develop, and attract visitors from all over the world, it will probably see an increase in hauntings. *Hauntings can become more prevalent with the influx of people to a given place or site. One reason is that the living sees them more frequently and talks about what they have seen. Another reason is that what was once left alone and forgotten is now reawakened to roam freely.*

Branson, Missouri has its ghosts, and it has many ghost stories. There is a haunting lurking just around the next corner!

Branson Bits

The Ghost of Cameron Mitchell

Cameron Mitchell (1918–1994) was a popular American film and television actor. He also appeared on Broadway. His career started in 1945 when he began appearing in movies; he played the role of Uncle Buck Cannon in the television series, "The High Chaparral," which ran 1967–1971 with ninety-seven episodes. Set in the American West, Uncle Buck Cannon was a perfect character for Mitchell and he excelled in his role.

A prolific film and television star, his character roles were varied and interesting. Here is a quick reference to some of his films from a long acting

Cameron Mitchell.

career: "They Were Expendable" (1945), "Bess" (1948), "Death of a Salesman" (1951), "Pony Soldier" (1952), "Les Miserables" (1952), "Garden of Evil" (1954), "House of Bamboo" (1955), "Love Me or Leave Me" (1955), "Carousel" (1956), "All Mine to Give" (1957), "Monkey On My Back" (1957, considered one of his best films), "Hombre" (1967), "The Midnight Man" (1974), and "The Tomb" (1986).

Cameron Mitchell's ghost has been seen at different restaurants and gift shops in Branson. He is seen wearing a dark business suit and smiling, and then he is gone. The ghost of Cameron Mitchell was first seen in Branson in the summer of 2000.

The Mists of White River

White River is noted for its early morning and early evening mists. They linger and play on the water and banks like wispy children from a fairy tale, each having its own shape and story to share. White River is also well known for its fine fishing, but there is a darker side to this old, long river as it makes its way across the land. There have been deaths and mysteries as yet unexplained connected with White River—over the decades, people and animals have vanished in this river.

Sightings of bobbing heads are often seen. People fishing have heard voices while they are on the water, but there is never any presence of the speakers. It's a magnificent, powerful river—one to enjoy, but one to also be wary of when you are in or on it.

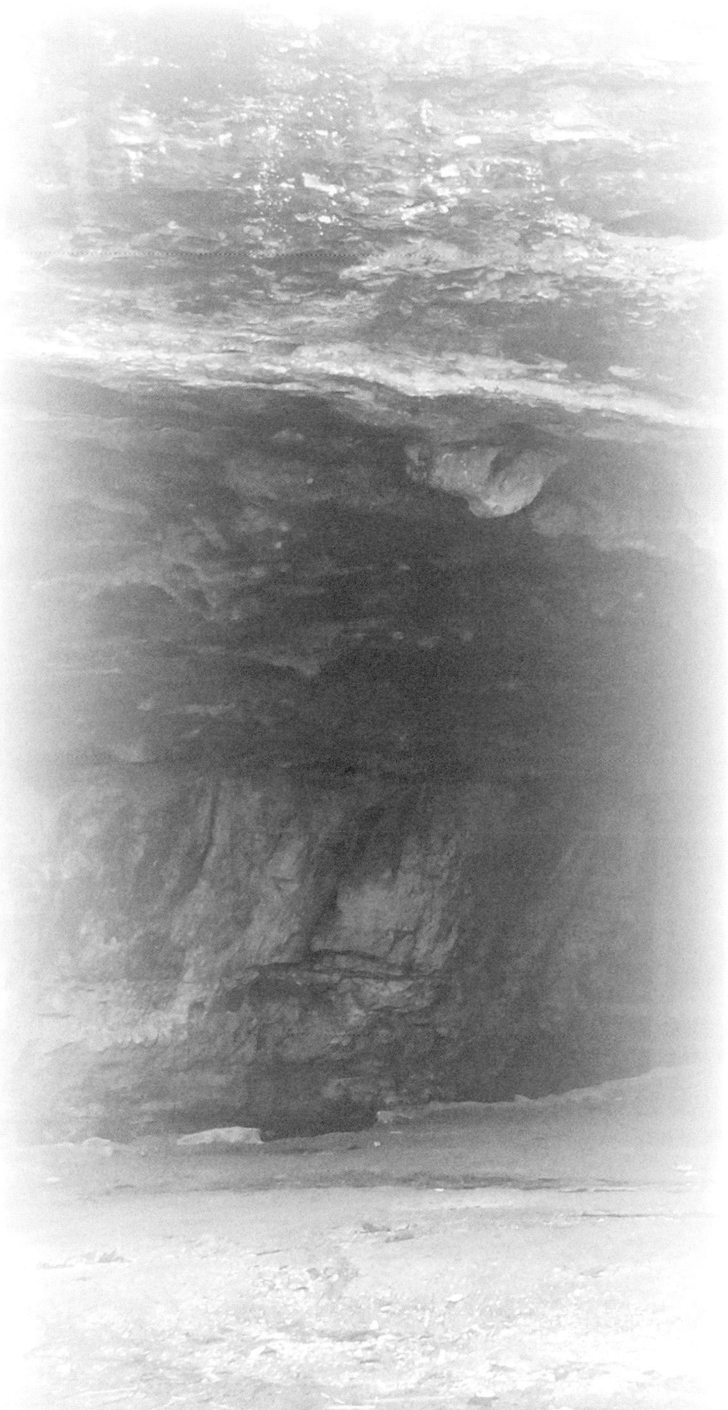

4

Chasing Ghosts in Chadwick, Missouri

Within Christian County is the town of Chadwick, Missouri, located in the Ozark hills with many caves and springs and approximately six miles southeast of Sparta, Missouri. Chadwick was a timber industry town and had the rough reputation of being a railroad stop with saloons and brothels. Gambling and violence were not uncommon in this area.

Bald Knobbers' Hanging Cave

The Bald Knobbers were a large group of vigilantes in Chadwick, Missouri. Non-racial in nature, this group took the law into their own hands and administered their own brand of justice. They wore dark hoods, which had holes cut out for their eyes, nose, and mouth. The hood had tied, peaked corners, which gave the wearer an appearance of being a horned avenger. Originating in Southern Missouri, they held sway during the decade of the 1880s. If there was a problem to be solved and the regular course of the law could not be done quickly enough, the Bald Knobbers solved the problem immediately. Shootings, beatings, and hangings were common.

Not far from the rural town of Chadwick, on Swan Cave Road, is a cave where hanging activity took place. There, the legendary Bald Knobbers hanged a man; the victim survived the first hanging and was then forced to repeat the hanging a second time. That time, the hanging killed him. His ghost haunts the location of his death, appearing at times to repeat his second hanging.

Today, Chadwick, Missouri is a small, quiet rural town surrounded by caves and springs. There is no hint of its rowdy Bald Knobbers past as you drive through it. The people are friendly when you visit with them, and if walking, a friendly wave or nod of the head is usually returned in like fashion.

And Other Hauntings...

Swan Cave Road has other haunting related stories separate from the Bald Knobbers. Shadow figures have been seen at twilight on the roadway. They seem to linger at the timberline, hesitant to move forward—and vanish upon approach.

5

Apparitions in Ash Grove, Missouri

Ash Grove, Missouri is a small, prosperous town with various businesses and historic sites. Some of the historical sites are Berry Cemetery (also known as the "Old Negro Cemetery"), which is listed on the National Register of Historic Sites; the Old Jail; the Ozarks Afro-American Heritage Museum; the Nathan Boone Homestead, which is another state historical site; and the Gilmore Octagonal Barn. The Berry Cemetery opened in 1875.

The Hauntings...

There is a story of the ghost of an elderly man who lingers near the Nathan Boone Homestead and seems to be watching or waiting for someone. He has been seen in the late afternoon, but fades from view on approach by the living. Shadow figures have been seen in the woods and other areas of the town.

If you have the time, give yourself a treat of a fine catfish meal and coffee at Fred's Fish House located at 123-A West Main Street. You won't be disappointed! While in the town, take a look around at the old buildings and enjoy the town's friendly atmosphere.

The Haunted Bridge

There was a well-traveled bridge in Ash Grove, Missouri. Built in 1926, the bridge was a three-span, open-spandrel arch structure set over the Sac River on U.S. Highway 160. Its original location was west of the town of Ash Grove. It was demolished in 2006, but shadow figures continue to live on where it once stood, unaware of the bridge being gone.

An interesting historical note about this area is that Ash Grove was the birthplace of the notorious 1930s criminal, Kate "Ma" Baker (1871–1935), although historically she was more an accomplice than actual member of the Barker–Karpis Gang. Her life was made into two movies, Roger Corman's "Bloody Mary" (1970) and Ken Russell's "Public Enemies" (1996).

6

Feeling the Spirits in Fair Grove, Missouri

Fair Grove, Missouri is a small town approximately fourteen miles from Springfield. Established in 1856, the town is noted for its gristmill built in 1883.

This gristmill is located at Old Mill Road (Highway 125) and Main Street, and was originally named the Boegel and Hine Mill. After many owners, it was last named the Wommack Mill. This old structure has been restored and is now listed as a Missouri Historical Site under its original name of Boegel and Hine Mill.

Ghost Bridge

Traveling along U.S. Highway 65 towards Fair Grove is an old bridge that passes over the Pomme de Terre River area. This abandoned bridge can be seen from the highway. Built in 1928, it was once a sturdy, well-traveled, three-span, open spandrel arch bridge.

The viewing of this once proud bridge is startling in its intensity. The crumbling bridge is reputed to be haunted by a headless ghost in search of its head.

Was this the result of a long ago accident, or some forgotten incident that happened during the American Civil War along the banks of the Pomme de Terre River? Did some hapless person, grown weary and tired, fall asleep on the bridge and awaken to foul play? Was a person murdered there and the body dumped off the bridge? A missing person's incident, long forgotten or lost in the paperwork files? Or perhaps nobody was aware of the death, the body, and severed head dumped off of the bridge, the remains absorbed by time and the elements? Is the ghost doomed to search for its head for eternity?

Mentally, take that one step beyond and give it your best haunting analysis! What do you think? Was this ghost a woman or a man? This headless ghost is said to haunt the ruined bridge on the nights of a full moon, when the wind is high and summer crickets sing loudest.

Part Six: Feeling the Spirits in Fair Grove, Missouri

Fairgrove haunted bridge, full view.

    This is a lonely abandoned bridge, and if you want to take pictures of it, the bridge will oblige you, allowing you to photograph it without interference! This bridge is alive with paranormal impressions and direct connections to ghosts. In fact, the first immediate contact my wife Debra and I received from the bridge was that it wanted the company of the living. A once magnificent bridge but now condemned, it was demolished by the state of Missouri in 2008.

    The bridge has also had its share of shadow figures on it—and these figures still haunt it. The shadow figures remained on the riverbanks and bluffs even after the bridge's demolition.

    When Debra and I visited this bridge together in February 2008, it was a pleasure to become open to the impressions as we slipped onto its ruined top surface. Debra's first impression was of an invisible, friendly presence pushing her gently down an incline from our parked car in the direction of the bridge. There was also a sad presence on the right side of the bridge, which made itself known to Debra; it was not a shadow figure, but a presence. We saw shadow figures on and under the bridge. Debra received distinct impressions of young children laughing and playing on the bridge and the riverbanks below.

    I was standing in the center of the bridge when something gently kissed my left cheek. Immediately, my mind's attention turned towards a concrete rectangular baluster at my feet. I examined it and felt an immediate, overpowering connection with the presence of a young woman wearing 1940s clothes; my impression of this ghost and my communion

Part Six: Feeling the Spirits in Fair Grove, Missouri

Fairgrove haunted bridge.

with her was distinct, spiritually intimate, and poignant. Those were the strong feelings she induced in me when she found me on the bridge. Her appearance was not in color images, but in muted gray tones like an old faded black and white photograph. She was pretty, petite, fair-complexioned, shoulder-length auburn hair, and her name was Cindy, which was my complete impression. She was actively seeking to make contact with me in a sincere manner, but I could not understand what she was saying because her words were not in sync and the clarity of her voice was wobbled. There was much emotion in her face while she attempted to communicate with me, and she seemed genuinely surprised and pleased that I could see her. Her presence lasted less than a minute and then was gone, carried away by the chill wind of this clear, beautiful, sunny afternoon.

Cindy was an intelligent haunting. I suspect she will be around that bridge and riverbanks area even though the bridge itself is destroyed.

Despite pieces of the bridge having been hauled away, I salvaged the ruined, rectangular

Shadow figures on bridge.

87

Part Six: Feeling the Spirits in Fair Grove, Missouri

Part Six: Feeling the Spirits in Fair Grove, Missouri

Lee Prosser in contact with ghost.

baluster at which Cindy made her ghostly appearance. That supernatural piece of memorbilia now rests at my residence near my flower garden—and has the presence of ghosts attached to it!

I took photographs of the bridge and also where shadow figures lurked; however, these shadow figures did not attempt to make direct contact with Debra or me. Both Debra and I felt that the shadow figures were present while we were there, and their presences were independent of any other impressions we encountered on the haunted bridge near Fair Grove, Missouri.

Haunted Highway 125

Highway 125 connecting Strafford, Missouri with Fair Grove is noted for some unusual paranormal activity. Stories of ghost hitchhikers who thumb a ride only to vanish when you drive past them are said to happen frequently.

Another story is about an older woman wearing 1880s western clothes and riding a big bay mare, who appears and then disappears, as if a door opens through which she and the horse enter together and then slowly closes behind them! A driverless, early style 1940s black Buick Sedan passes other cars in a hurry...only to vanish in the distance ahead without a trace.

Six dogs cross the highway at its midpoint around the noon hour — only to disappear in the middle of the highway. A smiling young man wearing 1960s clothes and a backpack appears at the side of the highway; he is talking to another unseen person, laughs, and then vanishes as if suddenly pushed or pulled backwards from the shoulder of the highway! Two blonde-haired women in their early thirties wearing blue jeans, white tennis shoes, windbreakers, and shouldering red backpacks are seen standing and talking along the left side shoulder of the highway, but on approach, the women vanish instantly...like a light bulb was turned off.

7

"Spirited" St. Louis, Missouri

Louis Jolliet and Father Jacques Marquette arrived in 1673. The French brought their unique ways and customs to the state and did much to actually settling early Missouri, and establishing a history for the state. In 1763, St. Louis was on its way to becoming a legend with the founding of a fur trading location by Pierre Laclede de Liguest.

Many historians credit August Chouteau as the true founder of St. Louis, as his influence at one time was felt throughout Missouri. Married to Clemence Coursault, they raised ten children including two sons, Henri and Gabriel. With time, the area became settled, and haunted.

Old vintage postcard of St. Louis, Missouri.

The Hauntings...

St. Louis had many fires and disasters, and there were also the plagues that came and went, leaving devastation in their paths. The city had its share of cholera epidemics with one such epidemic killing over 4,000 people in 1849.

The Great Cyclone of 1896 devastated parts of the city. Tornadoes of varying sizes and strengths killed many over the decades and took their toll of lives. Disasters both natural and unnatural have given the city paranormal happenings.

The Lemp Mansion, at 3322 de Menil Street, has been the talk of ghost hunters for years and its popularity as a haunted location with an abundance of paranormal activity keeps its reputation alive. Among the documented events to have occurred at the house is the fact Charles A. Lemp shot himself, along with his dog, in the basement in 1949. Sounds of voices, laughter, and water running have been heard; shadow figures haunt the house and grounds; and there is an invisible presence that touches people on the second floor. The ghostly sounds of a piano being played without a pianist is a story oftentimes told. A woman humming the music of a 1950s love ballad, Johnny Mathis' "Chances Are," has been heard in the house, but there is no sight of the woman humming this lovely song.

Women ghosts have been seen many times, and Julia Lemp is one of the reputed ghosts haunting the mansion. Charles Lemp is another ghost whose presence is most felt, and active.

Much has been written and told about this haunted home. The written documents available to the public are as numerous as the verbal accounts. Given the variety of people and their beliefs in the formative years of St. Louis, much is possible.

The Mississippi River

The Mississippi River and St. Louis have an involved and unique marriage; simply put, you cannot have one without the other! This river, like many rivers of its nature and murky depths, has its share of bobbing head stories and of people drowning in the river and their ghosts seen in the water. This, of course, includes the uncounted and unknown number of murder victims whose remains settled to the muddy bottom. Young pregnant women were also among the river's many victims who accepted the solitude of river suicide rather than the shame of being a fallen woman in those historical times. The river probably holds the remains of failed loves and lonely lovers more so than can be imagined. The Mississippi River holds many secrets, which includes the paranormal happenings in and around it since human settlement started.

Part Seven: "Spirited" St. Louis, Missouri

In 1874 a riverboat named *Iron Mountain* vanished with its cargo and passengers, and to this day, there are stories of French-speaking voices being heard by hikers and people fishing along the bank. Somewhere in time, that riverboat is still cruising the Mississippi River with its ghosts, but the living **WON'T** see it again. It's amazing that these residual hauntings from the riverboat passengers continue to haunt, but even more amazing are the times in which a person or group encounters the floating riverboat on a foggy river night. As long as there are ghost sightings, the *Iron Mountain* will be among them.

There are also accounts of the ghost of American author Mark Twain being seen walking the banks. Twain's connection with the Mississippi River and Missouri is well-documented in numerous sources, including his own travel writings, autobiographical works, and novels. He was an active member of the Society for Psychical Research and maintained an enduring interest in the paranormal throughout his life, and there are accounts of his psychic adventures. Readers would find his *Life on the Mississippi* and *The Stranger* interesting reading. There are many books by and about Mark Twain available and much can be found out about him and his prolific writings on the Internet and at the public library.

Jefferson Barracks National Cemetery

The impact of the American Civil War was an important factor in the city, and both the North and South fought for control of the city because of its major importance as a river city for transportation. Confederate spies, Union spies, murders, rapes, beatings, knifings, boat burnings, robberies, bombings, and abductions were frequent, further fueling the development of later paranormal activity.

Sabotage of the steamboat, *Sultana*, was typical of many of the burnings and sinkings that took place. There were an estimated sixty Union steamboats destroyed by the Confederates on the Mississippi River during the war, resulting in thousands of lives being lost. Is it any wonder that the Mississippi River has so many bobbing head ghost stories and ghost sightings?

Gratiot Street Prison at 8th and Gratiot Streets served as the Union prison for Confederate soldiers, although it also held other prisoners the Union wanted to imprison. This prison was unhealthy and subject to disease. It was demolished in 1878 and the Ralston Purina Company now stands in its place. Many people died at Gratiot Street Prison of small pox and related diseases. These bodies were usually taken for burial to the Jefferson Barracks National Cemetery at 2900 Sheridan Road. This cemetery is haunted by shadow figures, and voices have been heard. A ghost dog is said to roam the cemetery, but vanishes upon close approach; it has been described as a German Shepherd or a large collie. Ghost stories of American Civil War soldiers roaming the cemetery have been in circulation for decades. A thoughtful, quiet woman is seen at a grave in the west side of the cemetery, her face hidden and bowed as if in prayer. Is she praying for the soul of a deceased relative, or seeking to honor a past love when he was alive?

A young couple dressed in 1920s era clothing has also been seen standing near a gravesite in the east section of the cemetery. Are they seeking to visit a dead relative, or are they simply passing through to elsewhere? Upon approach, the couple stares towards the west and vanishes.

A stocky, elderly farmer wearing bib coveralls, boots, and a white undershirt, carrying a shovel, and accompanied by two beagle dogs is said to frequent the south side of the cemetery. This ghost farmer disappears upon approach. Is the farmer coming from a burial, or searching for his own plot of internment, one wonders?

Jefferson Barracks National Cemetery is one of the most haunted locations in the city of St. Louis and the more the area is examined, the more paranormal activity is unearthed. There are 135 acres, and the many buildings on this land carry their own ghostly tales of hauntings and sightings. Going back in time to the beginning of this military post, it is documented in numerous sources as having been the site for housing soldiers protecting settlers from American Indian attacks. Named after President Thomas Jefferson, the post itself was established on October 23, 1826.

There have been sightings of ghost children playing on the grounds; they will fade, vanish, and reappear at random times. A small boy, around eight years old, was once seen near the entrance of the Cemetery, but when approached, this little boy seemed to step into another dimension and close an invisible door behind him! Haunted sightings abound in this location. Some people have seen children who are playing together suddenly vanish into the thin air!

Two Confederate soldiers were seen near a structure and appeared to be singing and having a good time. They did not linger, but went on their way, vanishing around the corner of a building. Did these men come back to visit the place they where they were held prisoners or did they come back to visit the place where they both died? Were they friends in the same unit, captured, and held prisoner? What is the reason behind their lingering visit in time? Perhaps, they were in the same cell and became friends? There is always conjecture and questions concerning the origins of ghosts and that definitely includes the Jefferson Barracks National Cemetery.

Another haunting is that of a young man, in Union soldier dress, walking up and down in front of two graves, pointing first at one and then at the other. What is he trying to communicate? Does one grave contain this soldier's name and remains, or could an accident have taken place with his burial resting place being given to a wrong body instead!

A doctor carrying his physician's bag is seen hurrying along a well-worn path in the barracks...only to vanish in mid-air as he raises his left foot to take another, quick step! To what urgent business was he attending, or did he not make it soon enough to see that last patient on his round? What happened to this tall, bearded doctor who was in such a hurry?

When a person sees something out of the ordinary, he or she wonders what just happened and seeks some kind of rational answer. There are not always rational, logical, or self-explanatory answers for the appearance of ghosts and paranormal activity. If you are a sensitive, you look at these paranormal encounters differently than most other people do because that is what you do. Every situation is different for different people, although many times the same situation is witnessed by more than one person when the encounter happens. I make no claim to having answers.

But if you are not a sensitive, here is another possible approach to consider. Years ago I was told an interesting opinion about proving the existence of ghosts and paranormal activity that I wish to share with you. It went like this: *Proving that ghosts exist is like proving God created the earth in six days and rested on the seventh. You can't prove it, definitely. And you can't disprove it, definitely! You have to take it on trust and with a grain of salt. Take it on faith, or deny it ever happened, and go on! It is a personal choice and decision.* So my suggestion is that you record the paranormal encounter you had and share it with others! Just as living in the world of flesh and blood holds many surprises, so does paranormal activity in the afterlife.

We are not ever alone, for the dead are always with us in some form. That the Jefferson Barracks National Cemetery has an abiding and lengthy history of paranormal occurrences is no surprise, but a given fact. Ghosts are there, in abundance. But then, too, ghosts are in abundance everywhere!

Haunted Caves

Caves are always a possible location for ghosts and paranormal activity, some more so than others. Despite the best efforts of Hollywood movies, newly discovered caves do not necessarily have some evil thing lurking within them! But some caves do have residual hauntings. Possibly some have intelligent hauntings.

Any underground location that contains a cave or a maze of caves does have the possibility for incidents of the supernatural kind. I would suggest to you, the reader, that a fascinating book could be written about the paranormal connected with caves and it would be a very thick book. As to St. Louis, it does have caves.

The possibility that under the city of St. Louis is a maze of connecting and non-connecting caves is very likely. Historically, St. Louis beer makers used many caves and huge cavern areas for breweries. The Lemp family of St. Louis had such access to caverns and made ready use of the built-in coolness. Caves made for easy cool storage limited the spoilage of perishable goods. St. Louis is much like Springfield in the sense that both cities are built on caves—and there are more unknown caves than there are known ones.

I was told by three different people, including a geologist and a biologist, that for every known cave in Missouri there were at least five unknown, undiscovered, and forgotten caves still to be found. Other people have shared with me their educated guesses as to the possible number of caves still to be discovered in Missouri. There are a large number of unknown caves just waiting to be found....

Most of those caves will never be found, so I have been told. Alas, there goes my dream of one day owning a cave in Missouri! Although I am reasonably sure there is one somewhere deep beneath my feet and chair as I sit writing these very words!

The history of caves makes for a wonderful look at the ingenuity of humans putting caves to use over the many thousands of years. If there does come a climatic or terrorist holocaust, caves will be of prime importance for survival. If that becomes the case, humans should be aware that they would be sharing space with the ghosts of the cave's past to some degree, depending upon how haunted the cave is.

As to the underground cave system in St. Louis, there are some well-known caves. There is the Cherokee Cave—Adam Lemp used this cave for not only his personal use, but in connection with his brewery.

The passage of time and social changes resulted in the Cherokee Cave being sold and opened to the public for tours by a man named Lee Hess. Cherokee Cave held such sights as the Spaghetti Room and the Petrified Falls, but in 1961 the cave complex was sold to the Missouri Highway Department and permanently closed. But was it forgotten and no longer able to be entered? To the diehard cave searcher, no. There are ways into the cave. The Lemp Theater is still there among other relics in the cave. Haunted? Some say yes. Shadow figures are said to be there. What else, one wonders?

There are other caves in St. Louis. Among them is Uhrig's Cave, which served as a base for beer brewery operations. Another known cave used for brewery operations, now permanently sealed off from public access, is called the Sidney Street Cave.

English Cave, originally owned by Ezra O. English in 1826, is also a well-documented cave with a history of paranormal activity. English Cave was the site of the St. Louis Brewery in 1839. This cave is now filled with water and is inaccessible. English Cave is said to be haunted by different entities, including American Indians who once used the cave and victims of the cholera epidemic that devastated the city in 1849.

There is also a story told of a young couple who were in love and fled to English Cave and died inside it rather than be separated. The couple's ghosts are said to haunt the depths of English Cave with strange, eerie voices frequently heard. A feeling of the macabre permeates what is known as English Cave.

Other caves await discovery in St. Louis, Missouri. What is lurking inside them, I wonder?

Forest Park

Officially, Forest Park is larger than Central Park in New York City by over five hundred acres. Forest Park is a magnificent park visited frequently by people from all over the world—and it's haunted.

Forest Park contains many things to see and interact with...in addition to its hauntings. Like Central Park in New York City, Forest Park is one of the most photographed parks in the world. Attractions include the Old Footbridge, St. Louis Art Museum, Municipal Theater, St. Louis Science Center, Missouri History Museum, and the McDonnell Planetarium.

It is an easy park to find due to its immense size of approximately 1,371 acres, and is in the Highway Interstate 64, Kingshighway, Lindell Street, and Skinker Boulevard area. The vast area at South Kingshighway Boulevard, near Clayton Avenue, contains twenty lakes and ponds. One lake is said to have a small, white phantom boat with a woman

Old vintage postcard of Forest Park.

paddling the water towards a shore she never reaches! Another lake in the central section is said to have two bobbing heads that surface, submerge, and then do not reappear! Yet another lake is said to have a handsome male swimmer who seems to swim in tireless circles for a short time and then dives and does not resurface. Another lake setting has something that lurks just below its surface and makes waves as it swims under the water...but it's something that is never seen and nobody knows what it looks like.

Over the years, different areas have been considered for paranormal activity and ghosts. The boat dock at the zoo is where an elderly man walks the area and vanishes upon approach by the living; he is seen wearing a white dress suit with white vest and white tie and spats—and he appears in all seasons. Walking the Old Footbridge gives you an eerie feeling...there have been many stories of couples being seen to cross it and vanishing on the other side or near the middle of the bridge. Two young girls in long dresses are sometimes seen in the vicinity of the bridge, but they, too, vanish upon approach. An elderly woman in a gray 1950s woman's dress suit has been seen near the footbridge, most often at twilight when she appears momentarily and then disappears.

The St. Louis Art Museum has its share of shadow figures and ghosts that appear near the Pan statue and other art works. The Municipal Theater has its shadow figures and ghostly laughter. Different sites have had paranormal sightings over the years; these sightings have changed with the times, becoming more prevalent since the 1970s. Many sightings occur in the late afternoon and early twilight hours.

As a park to visit and walk, this is one of the finest in the world. A pleasant place, you will enjoy its atmosphere of charm and mellowness immediately upon entering its comfortable setting. Forest Park is the type of special setting that welcomes you with its open friendliness and solace.

Hospital Spectors...& Other Ghostly Sites

St. Louis Children's Hospital

Near what was called South Kings Highway Boulevard in the central west end of the city was the original Old St. Louis Children's Hospital. Built in 1944, it had over its lifetime reputed ghosts of children and nurses, on duty, walking the floors. The hospital was demolished.

Old City Hospital

This large, rambling, five-story hospital was founded in 1845, established to serve and help the indigent. In 1856 the hospital was destroyed by fire. There are several stories about an insane Italian who was rescued and then ran back into the fire to die and later became a ghost haunting the premises. He would sometimes be seen frantically exiting the hospital and then running, suddenly vanishing into a building wall. A residual haunting that was kept alive over the decades, rumors have it on clear nights he can still be seen fulfilling his death wish in the flames of long ago!

Construction commenced in different stages and the hospital, in its final form, was opened in 1905. The hospital was segregated, designed for whites only. Colored patients were dispatched to what was called Hospital 2 in the north part of the city. Problems at the Old City Hospital were numerous, and the reputation of the hospital self-destructed. Many deaths happened there.

Left unattended, the building fell into disrepair and was often the target of vandalism. Destroyed by progress, the setting is now in the process of becoming a location for condominiums.

Ghosts and entities of different types are reputed to haunt this immediate area. Moaning and screams are sometimes heard throughout the day and night. Crying and voices have been heard. Shadow figures frequented the location.

Homer G. Phillips Hospital

Originally known as City Hospital 2, it was located in the northern part of the city and was where all people with colored skin were sent for emergencies and medical care. It was a crude, oftentimes unhealthy situation for patients. Many deaths happened there. Replaced by an innovative, art deco setting and renamed the Homer G. Phillips Hospital in 1937, it became a respected hospital. This hospital had its share of ghosts and other entities walking the area, some seen outside the hospital and some inside the hospital. It's also one of the few hospitals in the United States to have an abundant number of legends and stories about involving black people.

Adams-Gehm House

Located in the 300 block of Plant Avenue is one of St. Louis' most haunted houses. Bart Adams built the house in 1890. From 1906 to 1944 a man named Henry Gehm inhabited it.

There have been numerous residual and intelligent hauntings in this house since the late 1940s. Voices have been heard. Various paranormal sightings including apparitions of men, women, and small children have been encountered. Shadow figures have been seen on the second floor... figures that seem to want contact with humans. The shadow figure of an older man has been seen at the front door entrance.

There have been stories of people being touched by invisible fingers. A woman's laughter has been heard in the kitchen. Footsteps on the stairs and throughout the house have been heard, but no walkers seen. The attic is reputed to be haunted by Henry Gehm himself.

Lafayette Square

Lafayette Square remains one of St. Louis' intriguing areas. Its history began in the early 1800s when the neighborhood became an area where the wealthy could settle. Over a period of thirty years the area was enlarged, and with additions to Lafayette Park, became a very desirable place to live.

By the late 1920s, it was no longer considered chic for the wealthy to live there. The area became a home for the working class and eventually slipped into a state of slums for the poor during and immediately after World War II.

Beginning in the late 1940s, successful efforts were undertaken to recapture the glory of this neighborhood and restore it. Stories of hauntings have been told over the decades, but nothing of a frightening manner. Shadow figures are reputed to haunt the area today, but their appearances are fleeting and diminishing in number...as if these ghostly shadows have become some particle of yesterday misplaced in time, not sure of the current surroundings and renovations.

8

Waking the Dead in Webster County

Marshfield, Missouri, was settled in the 1800s. Located in Webster County, the town has a certain charm that identifies it as a typical Missouri rural community with a friendly atmosphere. It is the birthplace of Edwin P. Hubble, who designed the Hubble Telescope, and is home to the Cherry Blossom Festival and the Webster County Museum.

Webster County has over sixty cemeteries, among them the Civil War Cemetery. It's been reported that orbs have been found in several of these old cemeteries, and stories of ghost have circulated for years regarding these sixty-plus cemeteries. There are many small towns of interest in Webster County.

Ghosts in the Rivers

Webster County is also home to several rivers. Its major city is Marshfield, located approximately seventeen miles east of Springfield. These rivers are the Niangua, Finely, James, Osage Fork, and Pomme de Terre. This area of Missouri was the location of American Civil War action between the North and South. The Union and Confederacy fought against each other, oftentimes using the same travel routes. Soldiers from both sides died here and some of their ghosts are still in the area. Some bodies were never found and some deaths were never recorded. In 1862, the telegraph line was established and ran near what became known as Old Wire Road, near Marshfield. Old Wire Road is reputed to be haunted with ghosts of Civil War soldiers from both sides. There have also been stories of orbs in the vicinity.

Stories about water ghosts have been told over the decades, as any river can and does attract stories about drownings. I have formulated a theory about these spectors of bobbing heads and floating bodies based on years of observation and research. Water ghosts, or bobbing heads and floating bodies, result from the impact of a drowning death and the drowned person being unaware that he or she has died. These hauntings can be residual or intelligent.

Tales of orbs and shadow figures on Highway 65 from Northview through Conway and Highway 38 from Marshfield to Elkland are frequent stories. The shadow figures appear alongside the highways during early evening when the light is fading and night is coming.

There is also a story of a singing woman who walked along the banks of the Osage River in the 1950s; her ghost was said to vanish upon approach.

As an important historical note, there were three groups of Native Americans living in this and nearby areas prior to the middle 1800s: Osage, Delaware, and Shawnee. The Osage Indians were there first, possibly as early as the late 1500s, and they considered the land highly sacred and had legends concerning its past. Prior to the middle 1800s, many Indians lived, died, and were buried in Webster and surrounding counties.

I have long held a high respect for the legends, paranormal aspects, and sacred ways of the American Indian. They have left an important positive imprint on this particular Missouri area of nature and wild scenic beauty! You can feel their friendly presence when you walk this land.

Webster County is scenic, protected by good spirits, quiet, friendly, and the air is refreshingly clean. Much of Webster County remains unexplored.

9

Fishing for Ghosts in Forsyth, Missouri

Forsyth, like much of Missouri, has its share of shadow people. As an American Civil War setting, it was a focal point of battle between the North and South because it was a river town for steamboats on White River. Many drownings have happened in White River.

During the Civil War, both the Union and the Confederacy occupied Forsyth. Because of its river location, it was seen as a worthy prize. On July 22, 1861, General Sweeny and his force of Union troops recaptured the town for the North with casualties and loss of lives at the local courthouse. Sweeney and his forces returned to Springfield, Missouri with their loot and souvenirs. But on April 22, 1863, Union soldiers set fire to the town of Forsyth and destroyed it so the Confederacy would not recapture it.

On December 19, 1885, the Bald Knobbers destroyed the rebuilt courthouse. All documents and saved records were lost. In July 1912, the county jail was under construction and today houses the White River Valley Historical Society. The town's present location was established and developed during the 1950s.

A friendly, sociable town, Forsyth holds two annual festivals, the Harvest Moon Festival and Classic Car Show and the Spring Craft Festival and Classic Car show. Charlie Haden, an important jazz musician, composer, and bandleader, grew up in Forsyth. He won several awards for his recordings including two Grammy Awards.

Swan Creek Arch Bridge

Swan Creek Arch Bridge is what is architecturally defined as an open-spandrel arch. It was built over Swan Creek on Old Highway US 160 near Forsyth, which is located in Taney County. M. E. Gillioz of Monett, Missouri built it for the state of Missouri in 1932.

The figures of a young couple have been seen at the top of the pier on the bridge, but flicker and vanish once seen by the human eye. Sightings of shadow figures have been seen on the bridge and along the crossover points at either end of the bridge.

An unusual, dense mist is sometimes seen at the base of this old bridge from the 1930s. The mist arrives in the early evening as twilight comes, and it seems to lay low and circle the bases of the bridge, as if waiting for night to befall the area.

Perhaps the mist is lurking there for some reason as yet unknown and waiting to be discovered. Mists can and often do hide things.

The Horseback Rider & Shadow Figures

The figure of a sleeping horseback rider in 1870s western clothing has been seen at the edge of the town's approach. The ghost is that of a man with a wide-brimmed cowboy hat.

Sightings of shadow figures in the town have also been seen. There are many ghost stories about Forsyth. At one time, this area was within the Osage Indian borders and was home to the Osage Indians.

An old town site, now named Shadow Rock Park, is known for its ghostly shadow figures.

10

Ghostly Happenings in Galena, Missouri

Galena, Missouri has been blessed with one of the most scenic wilderness locations found in Missouri. It is in a rugged, natural setting and is the designated seat of Stone County.

The Ghosts of Y-Bridge

The Y-Bridge was the original bridge to cross over the James River, as it was constructed to accommodate MO (Missouri) Highways 248 and 413.

The bridge is closed to traffic and has been placed on the National Register of Historic Places. Not far away, a newer bridge was constructed to carry traffic across the James River.

Shadow figures have been seen on the old bridge. A couple dressed in 1950s summer clothes has been seen on the bridge at twilight, as if walking across it, but the young man and young woman vanish before reaching the other side.

Ghost hunters should find this bridge and Stone County an interesting place to visit. There is much to be experienced, and learned, within this land area near the James River.

Green-Eyed Lady of Highway 248

I share this personal encounter I had with a ghost. It was not my first encounter and it certainly won't be the last with an intelligent haunting! In 2008 I was investigating numerous haunted sites in Missouri. One that remains fondly in my mind is this encounter a few miles past Galena, Missouri.

I saw a woman with green eyes and long black hair at the right side of the highway. She appeared to be watching me intently...just as I was watching her intently. She raised her hand as if waving, and the wind pulled at her blue denim work shirt and blue jeans, and ruffled her hair. But there was no wind blowing on my side of existence...only hers. This attractive woman was probably in her late twenties, dressed in the beatnik-style of the 1950s, and looked like a real-life character out of Jack Kerouac's novel, *On the Road*. She wore black boots.

As her outstretched hand slowly descended in my direction, she started to fade and within seconds no longer existed. I hope to meet this green-eyed lady on the highway again one day, and somehow, I have a gut feeling, also known as *Intuition*, that she will be there. I call her "Judy Strawberry." Why that name, I don't know, but it seems to fit her and the area I was in when this ghost encounter occurred.

Maybe you, too, will come upon this ghost. I feel she has a message to share; perhaps another time she will share it.

Following Your Intuition...

I suggest that anybody investigating or searching for hauntings not pass up any opportunity to look for an article or item left behind at a haunting site. It may be a clue to the ghost's identity, or it could also have some symbolic reference to the haunting site. Nothing should be overlooked when it comes to items found at such a location. Too many known stories to tell relate how a person or group is out having a hike or walk and come across some object that is possibly tied to the paranormal. Follow your intuition, for you may well be one of those people who discover such a precious object of paranormal contact! When it comes to paranormal contact, nothing is ever ruled out completely until all avenues are exhausted, and there are always aspects to be seriously considered.

I visited with a young woman who said she always attempted to not overlook things she found while out exploring haunted sites. She said that for her personally, the impressions she received by touch initially were the true ones. She said it was not unusual to get different readings from different items at the same location. I commented that all objects have vibrations, and she agreed, saying those vibrations were a historical record of a given place and time of the previous owner.

A sensitive, psychic, touch reader, intuitive, and medium all have one thing in common to some degree or another: *They rely on their spiritual senses as they make active connection with the paranormal world.* These senses are, with variations, *clairvoyance, clairaudience, clairsentience, and clairaugustine.* These are the senses generally referred to and discussed when the word extrasensory perception is mentioned.

Essentially, these words all come from the French language. I would define them in this manner. Each is perceived as a learnable technique, gift, blessing, or skill. **Clairvoyance** is the technique for being able to see ghosts or images related to the paranormal. **Clairaudience** is the technique used for hearing sounds or voices, or both, from a paranormal perspective. **Clairsentience** is the technique for revealing a message or information from the dead or a given paranormal situation. **Clairaugustine** is the technique for paranormal contact by way of smell and taste, such as smelling the odor of lavender face lotion at a haunting.

There are other words and definitions, but they are all variations of the aforementioned. An important paranormal tool I will share with you, my readers, is **psychometry**.

Psychometry is the technique used to discover the past history of an object by its vibrations, energy, spiritual attributes, or magnetic field. It is the approach to discovering the memories found within that object once possessed by another person by touching and handling that object.

My theory is that the past is not lost, but still exists on a spiritual realm. Psychometry is the method by which an individual can reach and connect with that past.

Psychometry is a natural skill available to anybody who wants to develop it. Like many of the known psychic skills, it can be learned. Personal intuition comes into play.

Intent is everything, and anything else is secondary when it comes to reading impressions. You must not have preconceived ideas about the object being examined, but take it as it is, and allow the impressions to unfold in your mind without interference. Much depends on the intent of a reader, for the item being examined may have more than one impression and usually does. Let it flow to you and see what unfolds!

For example, you discover an old ring or key in the dirt while digging. Four different people may have handled that ring or key. You clean it carefully, take a liking to it, and decide to wear or carry it. A person wishing to read the impressions of that ring or key will then have the impressions of the four past owners in addition to his or her own impression.

A sensitive to these impressions will allow herself, or himself, to be open to what comes with psychometry applied to an object. Practice truly does make perfect, and it certainly can be achieved with the technique of psychometry.

Ghosts do exist. Paranormal activity is a form of existential reality based on pre-existing sequences in time. Our day will come when we pass from human flesh into spirit. Then we may become our own best ghosts of some pre-existing sequence in time.

In the meantime, it's important to learn, discover, document, and share all the information you come into contact with regarding the paranormal, ghosts, and hauntings. Share with others what you find. Others will either believe or disbelieve your findings and that is true of anything you share in life.

Some believe, some do not believe. With the passage of time, I personally feel there are going to be more believers than disbelievers when it comes to the paranormal occurrences that happen around us constantly! There are more and more witnesses to such things who are willing to come forward, talk about their experiences, share their findings, and openly discuss their personal encounters.

Another Dead Woman... Picture Found in Bible

Traveling through the Galena and the surrounding countryside, there are some old tumbled-down houses and structures in the county that need further investigating. Some of these places are found by word of mouth. Others are so lost in the hillside that they have become shadows in time and forgotten.

I came across one that held special interest. The house was in shambles; an old thing, forgotten and beaten down into oblivion by the passage of decades. There was a set of collapsed stairs that once led somewhere, but were nothing now but splinters, nails, and remnants. I came across some old rotted books.

One of the books contained religious text, and upon opening it, I found an old, small envelope containing the faded vintage photo of a young woman. I stared into her eyes.

I received the impression that she died young in some manner, but those eyes...I extracted the photo from the middle of the book, left its envelope casket behind, and took her with with me.

Ghost hunting turns up most unusual items at times. Photographs, if salvagable, are always a treat since they are portals into a past moment of time. Looking at such things, it's sometimes overpoweringly poignant the feelings that a long dead face can stir in a present day viewer!

You wonder, and you ask yourself: Who were you? Were you living in the 1880s when times seemed clearer and more ordered? Why are your pensive eyes so sad, and what color were your eyes? What are you trying to share with me with that special look on your face? Who were you? Where were you? Did you die young? Were you a flu victim, possibly, of the World War I era? What kind of dreams and aspirations did you have? So many questions, but, alas, they're only questions.

So, you file away that photo in your hand, and come back to it another time, and again, you wonder at this ghost and ask the questions anew. Ghosts are everywhere.

Vintage photos are reminders of what went before. One wonders...

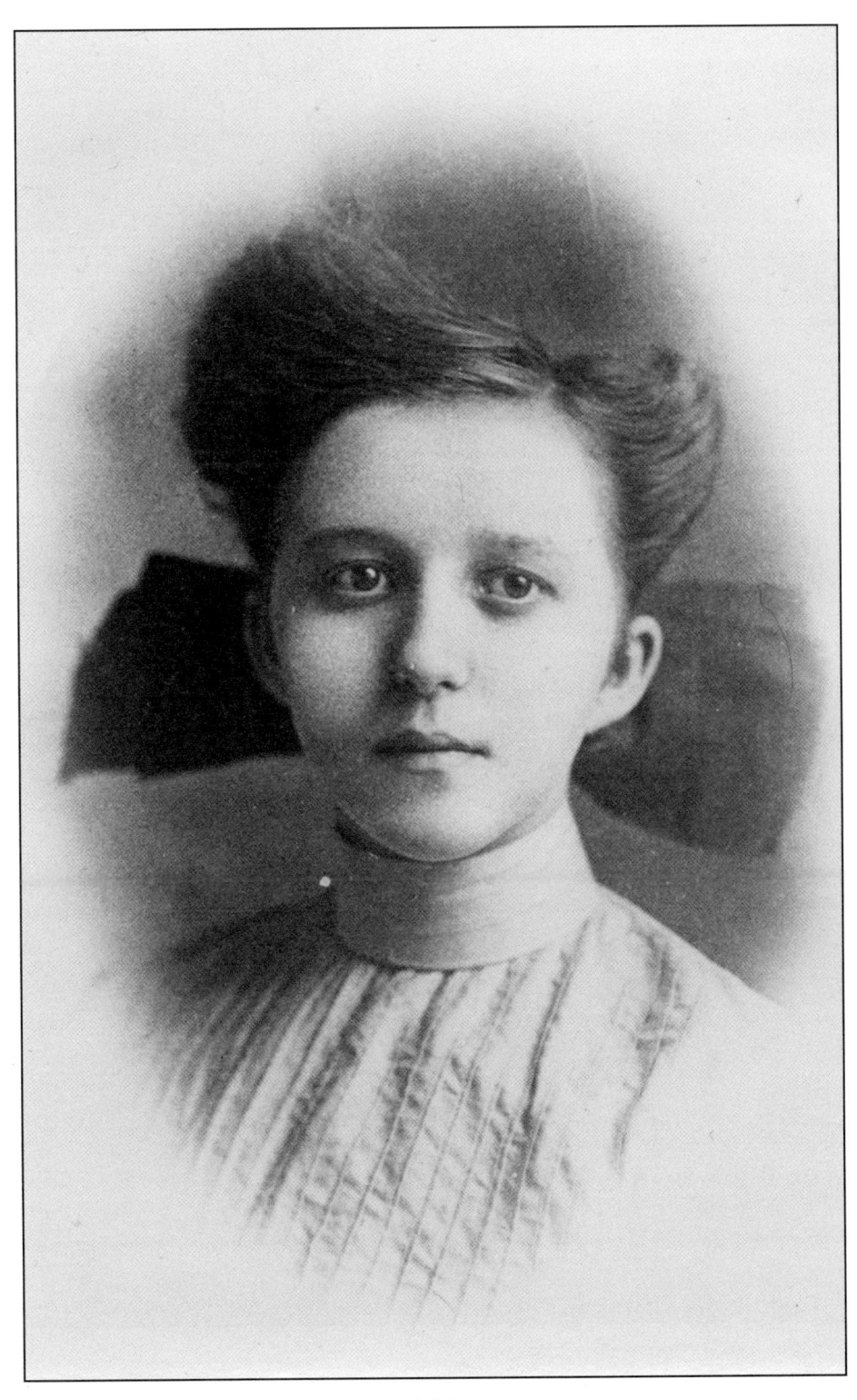

Part Ten: Ghostly Happenings in Galena, Missouri

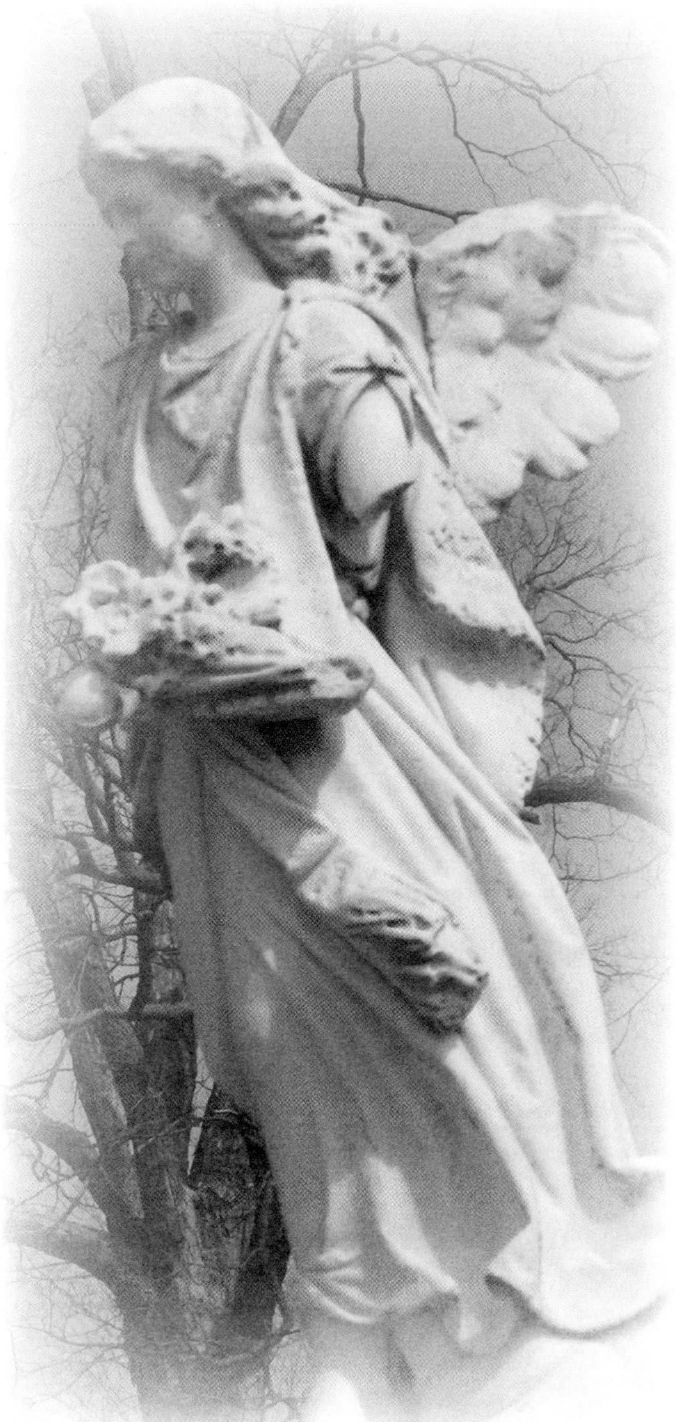

11

Haunted Hannibal, Missouri

Hannibal, Missouri is where Mark Twain (Samuel Clemens, 1835-1910) spent his youth, and is a nice city with a lot to see. The city was founded by Moses Bates in 1819 and has a long history of hauntings. Hannibal was the setting for Twain's two novels, *The Adventures of Huckleberry Finn* and *The Adventures of Tom Sawyer*. Among the city sights are the many ghosts....

The Hauntings...

One of the main attractions is the haunted Rockcliffe Mansion located on a knoll overlooking the Mississippi River. This mansion, now listed as a national historic site, has been called an American castle with its immense size of 13,500 square feet and thirty rooms.

When construction was finished in 1900, the owner moved in and established residence. He died in the mansion in 1924 and the mansion remained empty for years, not reopened until 1967.

Constructed as a showpiece mansion by wealthy lumber businessman John J. Cruikshank for himself, his wife, and their four daughters, Rockcliffe Mansion is haunted by Cruikshank. Other ghosts are also said to inhabit Rockcliffe, as different people have had many sightings and made reports of the ghosts.

Cameron Cave and Mark Twain Cave are haunted. Shadow figures and orbs have been seen inside and outside both caves. Cameron Cave has 260 passages and runs six miles in length. It's what is defined as a maze cave due to its winding structure.

Orbs, shadow figures, and the ghost of a haggard elderly woman have been seen at the Old Baptist Cemetery. Mt. Olivet Cemetery also has orbs and there have been sounds of macabre laughter there.

The ghost of wealthy businessman Albert Pettibone, Jr. is reputed to haunt the Garden House Bed & Breakfast. A grisly murder by ax decapitation fuels the flames of another famous haunting, that of murder victim Amos J. Stillwell in 1888. He was decapitated while in bed with his wife. The restless spirit of Stillwell is said to haunt the area in search of justice for his murder.

Another haunting is also related to a murder. A father believed one of his children was possessed by the devil. He took his eight-year-old daughter, held her down, and cut out her beating heart. He drank the blood for self-protection against the devil and demons. He was judged insane.

The father's ghost is said to haunt the south section of Hannibal, appearing only in the summer months. His mouth, face, and clothes are smeared with the bright red blood of his daughter whom he murdered, and he is said to be looking for his other children. This murder took place in 1869.

There are stories about restless American Indian ghosts haunting the hills near the city. A figure on a ghostly horse has been sighted and is the lost spirit of an Indian warrior killed in a fight and unable to find his way home. A banshee type of ghost is said to haunt the hills of Hannibal during the fall season and her screams are heard around the midnight hour. Her appearance eludes ghost hunters who have attempted to track her voice to its source.

Hannibal is definitely a stopping place for those interested in the paranormal. Tours of the Rockcliffe Mansion and other areas of Hannibal are available. One good time to visit this intriguing city is during October, which gives the visitor an opportunity to encounter the scenery and beauty of the area and walk the paths of fictional character Huckleberry Finn.

This seems like a nice place for the ghost of Mark Twain to visit, too, since he enjoyed exploring the cave named after him. In fact, Mark Twain is said to have held a life-long fascination for the cave.

A friendly city, you won't be disappointed having a stopover here in search of ghosts, the paranormal, and a good old-fashioned Missouri breakfast of ham, eggs, pancakes, sausage, hash browns, hot cocoa or coffee, and toast.

12

Mystic Monett, Missouri

Monett was originally named Plymouth Crossing and is approximately forty-two miles southwest of Springfield, Missouri. Established in 1887 as a railroad town, it has its collection of hauntings and ghost stories.

The Monett City Hall was built by M. E. Gillioz in 1929, and its two movie theaters were the Gillioz Theater and the Dreamland Theater. Both theaters were demolished years ago. The Gillioz Theater was noted for its architectural and interior beauty.

The Ghost of Robert Mitchum

Robert Mitchum (1917–1997) was one of the most popular actors in American film history. Popular worldwide, his numerous movies made money at the box office and included "Cry Havoc" (1943), "The Story of G.I. Joe" (1945), "The Red Pony" (1949), "River of No Return" (1954), "Track of the Cat" (1954), "Thunder Road" (1958), "Home from the Hill" (1960), "The Sundowners" (1960), "Cape Fear" (1962), "Ryan's Daughter" (1970), and "Dead Man" (1995).

Mitchum was an outdoors person who enjoyed nature and hunting. He frequently came to Missouri for hunting. The Monett area of wilderness was among his stops as well as other areas of Missouri.

There have been stories about Robert Mitchum being seen by hunters throughout Southern Missouri, which remained one of his favorite hunting haunts when he was alive. It appears Mitchum has carried that hunting hobby over into the afterlife!

In Southern Missouri, there are stories of ghost hunters appearing and then vanishing. Some appearances have involved intelligent hauntings while others have been residual hauntings.

The Gillioz Theater

The Gillioz Theater in Monett was a showcase theater at one time in its history. It was noted for its beauty and exquisite, colonial-style interior designs. It was also the meeting place for many a family wanting to have a night out at the movies. It was located at 520 Broadway Street. M. E. Gillioz, a resident of Monett and a wealthy road and bridge contractor, built it.

There are stories concerning ghostly voices being heard in the theater. A ghostly trio of young women was heard laughing and talking with two men in the main lobby of the theater, although there were no bodies to accompany the voices.

The Gillioz was an important feature of early Monett life, and a landmark building. It was later razed and the rubble hauled away to the landfill.

13

Spectors in St. Charles, Missouri

St. Charles, Missouri is a fascinating city with a history of hauntings. This is a city that deserves a full day's visit or even a couple of days—you will not be disappointed in what you find, learn about, and enjoy.

St. Charles is on the Missouri River and was founded in 1765 by the Frenchman, Louis Blanchette. Originally, the city was called "Les Petites Cotes," which, translated from the French language, means "The Little Hills."

For an enjoyable sense of walking back into a historical era, take a leisurely stroll down Main Street. Main Street is preserved from the 1800s and has much to offer the visitor in way of historical sites, gift shops, and restaurants.

The Hauntings...

Everybody I encountered could share a ghost story. There are stories of shadow figures seen frequently, and stories of men and women who prowl the city. Some ghosts appear in the clothes of the era in which they lived, others appear in white gowns, and some have been seen riding ghost horses. In the case of most of these residual hauntings, when they do happen, the paranormal outcome is that they appear briefly and disappear even more quickly.

There are many sites considered as hotbeds for paranormal activity and ghosts. Located on the Missouri River, there are the stories of bobbing heads that appear on the water, submerge, and never reappear. There is a ghost story about a couple with their baby clinging to their overturned flat boat as it floats down the Missouri River; they are seen for a time and then vanish as the boat seems to lift and sink beneath the water, taking the three humans with it to a watery grave. Another story involves a wounded, bleeding Union soldier carrying a fellow Union soldier over his shoulder, trying to make his way down to the edge of the river, going away from the city. The ghost of a young woman

Part Thirteen: Spectors in St. Charles, Missouri

with a young boy was seen along the edge of the river waving and then vanishing in a morning mist.

There are houses that are haunted, too. Among them is the legendary Poindexter Home built on Jefferson Street in 1855. The Poindexter Home is well known for its paranormal activities and numerous hauntings. Much has been written about its ghostly inhabitants.

Lindenwood College is another well-known place for paranormal activity, and may have served indirectly as an inspiration for some ghost movies. This is an educational setting you will be interested in visiting, as an onsite examination of this old college will turn up some unusual findings. There is a feeling of history about this place—one that you should be able to connect with once you are walking its grounds. The sense of the past is with you as you walk about the area.

Poindexter Home and Lindenwood College are said to be haunted by both residual and intelligent hauntings. St. Charles, Missouri is a place where the paranormal makes its home!

On the River...

Haunted Steamboat

St. Charles, Missouri is a river town located beside the Missouri River and is within twenty-five miles of St. Louis, Missouri. The *Goldenrod Showboat* is an old steamboat located at 1000 South Riverside Drive. It has become a popular dinner theater over the years.

During its active use as a river steamboat, the daughter of the boat's captain was found drowned. This young, beautiful woman is said to haunt the showboat in a friendly fashion, and there have been many sightings of her. An elderly couple has also been seen; they seem to be viewing something and then evaporate into the night mists.

More infrequently, a cat's meow is heard, but nobody has ever seen a cat anywhere. Voices without bodies have also been heard.

Missouri River

The Missouri River has its abundance of ghostly bobbing heads that surface, submerge, and disappear completely beneath the dark waters. Shadow figures have been seen along its banks and near buildings and structures along the bank.

Given this river's haunted history, it's probably more darker with long-forgotten deeds than is known. The Missouri River harbors many secrets in its cold depths.

14

Seeing Things in St. Genevieve, Missouri

St. Genevieve is one of Missouri's oldest settlements, and has a history dating back to 1735 when it was founded as a French colonial village. Located in Southeast Missouri, it's a lovely town that sits on the banks of the Mississippi River.

It has had numerous hauntings over the past two centuries, and these supernatural occurrences have included intelligent and residual hauntings. Some of the hauntings include the presence of orbs, ghost sightings, shadow figures, animals, voices, and cemetery hauntings.

St. Genevieve is one of the finest examples of what a French colonial village looked like in the early 1700s. Part of the town's history includes the robbery, on May 27, 1873, of the St. Genevieve Savings Association by Jesse and Frank James, and Cole Younger and his outlaw gang. This wild bunch of robbers succeeded in stealing $4,000 dollars for its gang members!

A charming, friendly town to visit, it is an enjoyable place for eating a good lunch of roast beef, vegetables, homemade pudding, apple pie, followed by some fine, strong coffee. Everybody I talked with had a ghost story to share. Some of those stories are listed elsewhere in this book. There is much to see in this colorful, historical town. The charm of the town is reflected in the care by which the inhabitants maintain their homes, streets, and town.

Haunted Houses, Taverns, & Cemeteries

Augustin Aubuchon – Therese Lalumondiere House

An interesting structure, it was built in 1785. Orbs have been seen. The ghost of an elderly man in a 1930s three-piece brown suit has been seen. He wears a brown derby hat and white spats on his dark shoes.

Beauvais – Amoureux House

The Beauvais – Amoureux House has orbs.
There is also the figure of an elderly woman in a long white dress seen at the outside of the front door during cold winter nights. This woman seems locked out and trying to get back inside the house for warmth. She is seen to knock on the door before vanishing.

Bequette – Ribault House

A ghost dog, perhaps a collie, roams the premises, but vanishes on approach. Orbs have been seen at the rear of the structure.
A young girl ghost, approximately ten years old, wearing early 1900s clothing, appears during the summer months on weekends. She's playing with a striped cat.

Bolduc – Le Meilleur House

An elderly couple dressed in early 1900s clothing visits the structure and then walks on, disappearing into the night. The couple seems to be walking the neighborhood. The man has his arm inside the woman's arm as they walk along.

Guibord – Valle House

An interesting structure with an interesting history of hauntings. The house was built in 1806. Stories of orbs, ghost sightings, voices, noises, and shadow figures have been reputed to be associated with this house. The voice of a young boy is heard calling his mother. The sound of gurgling is heard near the rear of the house.

The sound of running feet comes up to the front door entrance and then suddenly stops as if anticipating some person will open the door to the runner. Soft sighs have been heard near the left rear side of the structure, and a woman's voice gently saying, "Henry, Henry..." A meowing cat has been heard near the front door entrance.

A young woman is seen looking out a front window, her face sad and lonely. Two ghost dogs have been seen patrolling the house, circling it, as if looking for somebody, but upon approach they vanish.

Jean Baptiste Valle House

Built in 1794, the house is said to be haunted by a woman wearing a long red dress and a red bonnet with a large blue ribbon around its brim. I did not sense her presence at the time I was near the structure. I think it would have been interesting to see her and determine if she is a residual or an intelligent haunting. Perhaps, another time she will make her presence known to me.

Orbs have been seen here. The sound of a woman singing has been heard.

I noticed only a refreshing breeze and a bird singing sweetly in the background, but no presences.

To open yourself up, to be able to sense and receive, is not a difficult thing to do once you learn and understand how it works. I would suggest to those interested in opening themselves up to a given scene and situation for spirit or paranormal contact to be aware you may receive more than you bargain for. The easiest way to turn off paranormal reception is to ground yourself and take your mind elsewhere onto more mundane matters at hand, concentrate only on them.

Some individuals are capable of astral traveling to a given location or scene and becoming sensitized to the paranormal existing there. Also, the fine art of trained astral training is virtually the same approach as what is used for remote viewing techniques. The United States government has used remote viewing for spying and finding classified locations for a very long time now, so this should not surprise anybody!

There are plenty of books available on both astral travel and remote viewing to satisfy curious readers. Any person can do it with training. You may want to look over the books *Mastering Astral Projection: 90-Day Guide to Out-of-the-Body Experience* by Robert Bruce and Brian Mercer, and *Remote Viewing Secrets: A Handbook* by Joseph McMoneagle.

Greentree Tavern

Orbs have been seen frequently. Different variations of male ghosts appear, seem to enter the structure, and vanish. Ghost appearances seem most frequent during the winter months, although some have been seen at other times.

A gray cat ghost is said to watch the tavern, sometimes sitting near the entrance door, but disappears upon approach. The historical name for this structure is the Nicholas Janes & Janis-Zigler House.

Labruyere House

Now called the Ratte – Hoffman House, the structure was built in 1784. This house is in disrepair and needs much renovation. Shadow figures and the ghost of a young woman in long blue dress have been seen here. Orbs appear in the early spring, but at no other time. A pinto ghost horse is said to prowl the front area near the house, but never approaches the house itself. The horse is a residual haunting.

There is a story of an old woman in a gray robe, who comes out on nights of the full moon and points her walking cane to the moon and speaks words, but no sound comes from her throat. Shadow figures have been seen in the upstairs windows. A young boy is seen waving from the upstairs right-side window.

St. Genevieve Memorial Cemetery

No visit to St. Genevieve is complete without a visit to the Memorial Cemetery. In use from 1787 through 1880, the cemetery contains over 4,000 buried bodies. In 2008, only 275 grave markers and tombstones still exist to note burial sites. There is a quiet feeling to this place, and it has that impression of quietness that comes with the paranormal. You may sense something, but you are not really sure what it is, or who is walking beside you from the other side.

There are presences in this cemetery, and I suggest there is the possibility of having intelligent haunting contacts—if you actively seek them. This cemetery has old spirits, friendly ones, that are simply curious.

Orbs have been seen. Ghost animals have been seen, most notably, cats. Shadow figures are always present, but recede on approach and fade away.

An interesting place, study the burial markers and take in the history of this friendly spot between two worlds. When you visit this cemetery, linger a while at the following burial sites and see what impressions you receive: the burial sites of Marie Louise Valle (1798–1827), Jean Baptiste DeLafonte (1739–1790), and Charlotte LaCourse (1740–1788).

15

Haunted Joplin, Missouri

The Hauntings...

Joplin, Missouri is the location of many hauntings and has a long, colorful history. Growing up in Missouri, I heard many unusual stories about hauntings and ghosts in Joplin.

Located in the southwestern corner of Missouri, the city of Joplin was at one time considered the lead and zinc capital of the world. It was named after Reverend Harris Joplin who founded the first major Methodist congregation and church in the city. Lead mining started before the

Old vintage postcard of Joplin, Missouri

American Civil War, and by 1871 there was a large abundance of mining camps in operation. Joplin became recognized as a city in 1873.

Bonnie and Clyde lived in a hideout in Joplin for several weeks during the 1930s, which included their robbing several local businesses, but their stay ended in a shoot out. This famous outlaw couple escaped Joplin without injury. Stories of the ghostly presences of Bonnie and Clyde in Joplin still circulate.

Robert Cummings (1910–1990) was a famous actor from Joplin, as was actor Dennis Weaver (1924–2006). Famous writer and poet Langston Hughes (1902–1967) came from Joplin.

Situated at an elevation of approximately 1,011 feet on thirty square miles of land, Joplin is a good-sized city with a large population. Mining was discontinued in the late 1940s and mining operations completely closed down in the early 1950s, with the maze of tunnels abandoned.

One intriguing aspect of Joplin is the startling fact that tunnels beneath the city undermines seventy-five percent of its land, houses, buildings, structures, and streets. These old mine tunnels still exist although the majority of them are permanently closed. It's not uncommon to discover houses whose basements have a door opening into a mine for which the miner could come and go at random, going to work and returning home from work. Most of these entrances to mine tunnels are closed or permanently sealed, but they are still intact to some degree.

That these tunnels are haunted and have paranormal activity is something most ghost hunters would like to investigate more openly. Yet, the risk of mine cave-ins and other problems now existing with these old tunnels, mine shafts, and mines make it a very hazardous undertaking that has not been done. The passage of time has done much to permanently make these mines off limits for paranormal explorations. Oronogo and Webb City are two small towns close to Joplin noted for mines and tunnels.

A massive tornado struck Joplin on May 5, 1971. The center of the city was devastated.

Joplin is famous for some of its structures, among them, the House of Lords, which was a famous saloon containing a restaurant area, gambling tables, and an active upper floor used for prostitution and other sexual pursuits. Other interesting places include the SchifferDecker House built in 1890 and the Joplin Supply Company building.

There are haunted places in this old mining town, and its rough and rowdy early history adds to its appeal. Today, Joplin is noted for its friendly atmosphere and good meals. I would suggest the visitor try one of the restaurants offering roast beef, scalloped potatoes in gravy sauce, French green beans, sourdough toast, coffee, and apple pie or home-made bread pudding with vanilla sauce. It's always been a joy to visit Joplin when the opportunity presented itself.

The Ghost of Billy the Kid

The lonely ghost of New Mexico outlaw, Billy the Kid, is reputed to be seen riding near the outskirts of Joplin, Missouri alongside Highway 44. The horseback rider is heading towards Miami, Oklahoma, and he is seen riding alone on a brown horse at a leisurely pace. There is no emotion in his face and he is staring straight ahead. Since Billy the Kid's relatives came from Missouri, there may be more to this connection than is known at this time. I have a personal theory that could explain such a haunting.

I have a paranormal concept, or theory, I'd like to share with you. It's based on ideas I have formulated over the decades concerning human bloodlines, and what I have seen, been told about, or witnessed. I call it my **Blood Haunting Theory**; it's defined as: *Blood Haunting is a haunting carried down through the blood lines of an individual until some force knowingly or unknowingly corrects, or eliminates it.*

What actions did Billy the Kid's relatives take, what deeds did they do that lived on after them, and in what ways did they carry out these actions? Billy the Kid is permanently etched into the American Wild West consciousness and Missouri is an intricate, intimate part of the Wild West mythology. It is something to consider.

Most readers are aware of Billy the Kid's legend, his role in New Mexico history as one of that state's most famous outlaws, his attraction to women, and his beloved nickname by the Southwest Spanish settlements as El Chivato who saw him as a hero of the oppressed.

Billy the Kid achieved an enduring place in western lore and outlaw mythology during his short, action-packed life. He was always being seen somewhere and was usually safe in the last place the law would think to look for him. This is an interesting aspect of being a well-known outlaw during Western times, and even today — somebody somewhere is always seeing the outlaw at sometime with someone! In much the same manner as Missouri's Jesse James and his brother Frank James, Billy the Kid had a knack for being in thirty different locations at the same time! Such is the stuff legends are made of. The killing of Billy the Kid took place on a quiet, warm July night in 1881.

Billy the Kid died at the home of his friend, Pete Maxwell, in Fort Sumner, New Mexico when he was fatally shot in the heart by his friend, Sheriff Pat Garrett. Billy had no revolvers on him and was unarmed, which made his murder easy to accomplish without a shoot out.

Many sources suggest that Billy the Kid was visiting his pregnant girlfriend, Paulita Maxwell, at the time of his midnight death. Much like the enduring tradition of Missouri outlaw Jesse James, the life of Billy the Kid is the stuff of which great western legends, tales, and myths are made of. Jesse and Billy's ghosts, and their individual hauntings, will be with us for as long as people remember the American Wild West era and its oftentimes violent, lawless history.

When my wife Debra and I lived in New Mexico, we had the opportunity to visit the many ghost towns and haunted sites there. The residents call their state the land of enchantment, and that it is. It was always a pleasure for Debra and I to make trips to and through Lincoln, New Mexico, where Billy the Kid had one of his major shootouts. I believe it is true when one old-timer told me in a serious voice with a glint in her elderly blue eyes: "There is a piece of Billy the Kid everywhere you go in New Mexico. He knew what he was doing when he died here!"

Old vintage photograph of Billy the Kid.

There seems to be a piece of Billy the Kid and Jesse James everywhere you go in New Mexico and Missouri, respectively. Keep that intriguing thought in mind when you visit those states!

Joplin Hotspots

Connor Hotel

Completed and open for full occupancy in 1908, the Connor Hotel was an exquisitely designed hotel, both on the inside and the outside. It had eight stories and was the talk of Joplin.

There were reputed hauntings on the sixth, seventh, and eighth floors. These appear to have been residual hauntings from probably previous guests who left their imprint on time. The Connor Hotel was demolished.

Fox Theater

Originally called the Electric Theater, this old theater is still intact, listed on the National Register of Historic Places, and very much in use. Located at 415 South Main Street, it is now a pleasant church setting for the Central Assembly Christian Life Center. This theater is in remarkable shape, its Spanish Revival style and terra cotta lovely to look at.

Shadow figures have been seen around its entrance during the evening hours, but they come and go like a light bulb blinking on and off. Orbs have been seen at night floating near the entrance of the structure.

Joplin Supply Company

Joplin Supply Company is an old building with a long history in the city. It's reputed to have a woman's ghost on the fourth floor. The ghost of a pretty young child has also been seen staring out of a second floor window, and she is smiling.

Schifferdecker Home

This home was built in 1890 and is in excellent shape. Orbs have been seen in the attic room windows. A shadow figure, much like a man, has also been seen in the attic. Voices have been heard in the house, but no bodies have been seen to connect with those voices. An interesting place, it makes for a unique visit. There is a pleasant feel about the house.

Shoal Creek

Shoal Creek and the Grand Falls area are haunted. A band of American Indians on a hunting expedition has been seen. An American Indian riding a brown horse is reputed to appear at different places along the creek banks, as if studying the terrain or searching for something on the ground. Perhaps, he is tracking an animal or in pursuit of a person.

Shadow figures have appeared near the banks of the creek, only to step back and vanish at the approach of humans. Bobbing heads have been seen in the water. These bobbing heads submerge and do not resurface. Two heads of young men have been seen, but vanish on approach.

A young black-haired woman with fair complexion is seen floating on her back; she is wearing a one-piece red swimming suit and seems to be resting. On closer examination, she vanishes below the surface, fades away, and is not seen again.

Wildcat Glades Park

Wildcat Glades Park is a lovely, scenic park setting. There is a sense of the quiet here that is breathtaking and relaxing. Opened fully to the public in 2007, in what is called the Wild Cat Park contains trails for hikers to explore. It is a nature center for conservation, and an Audubon Center due to its variety of bird species.

It has shadow figures. A white ghost horse is said to prowl its boundaries. The ghost horse carries the ghost of a young girl wearing a long white dress.

Laughter without a presence to be seen has occurred. This laughter appears in the western section of the Park. It is the sound of a male ghost and has a throaty tone.

16

Haunted Kansas City, Missouri

Kansas City, Missouri is one of the most haunted cities in the United States, and its stories of hauntings, ghost appearances, and paranormal activity is legend. To those who live, prosper, and love the city, there is much to see and do in addition to the paranormal.

Set in rolling hills, the city overlooks waterways including the Missouri River. Noted for its blues and jazz music, it attracts many visitors to such festivals and performances.

Kansas City was a hotbed of gangster activity during the 1920s and 1930s. It is the heart and soul of what has become known as Kansas City jazz stylings, which have been popular since the 1920s. Restaurants and theaters are another cultural aspect for Kansas City.

The Hauntings...

Kansas City is a force unto itself, and the largest city in the state of Missouri. Founded in 1838, it became a city during 1850 and was named in 1889. American Civil War battles were fought in and around the city for its control. As an active slave state with strong sympathies toward the South, Kansas City sought to further the Confederate cause, but at the Battle of Westport in 1864 the Union victory ended the Confederate effort to occupy the city. Both the Union and the South saw Kansas City as a prize jewel to possess during the American Civil War.

It is not unusual to hear stories of Union and Confederate ghosts being seen in and around the city. These seem to be residual hauntings as no intelligent haunting contacts have been documented.

Walnut Street in downtown Kansas City is haunted, and many of its old buildings have been visited by ghosts and have had other paranormal activity. Near the sites of Union Station and the Liberty Memorial have been hauntings. World War II soldiers in uniform have also been seen at Union Station.

Old vintage postcard of Kansas City, Missouri.

Christian Church Hospital

Among the most haunted buildings in Kansas City is the Christian Church Hospital located at 2524 West Paseo Boulevard. Construction got underway in 1914 and the hospital was opened in 1916. Designed by architect Henry F. Holt in the Classic Revival Style, this sturdy, old, many-storied hospital served the community well during its lifetime, and was known to take care of the poor. Many of the victims of the World War I flu epidemic died there, brought in from all over the Kansas City area for treatment.

The hospital was once a veteran's hospital. It changed owners and there were periods of time when it was closed down.

At one point it was reopened as a mental hospital where experimental treatments were carried out. Prefrontal lobotomies were performed as often as fifteen times a week. An ice pick was used in most of the lobotomies rather than a scalpel. Prefrontal Lobotomy was often seen as a cure-all for various forms of mental illness from the 1920s throughout the 1950s.

Again the hospital was shut down and left empty. And again...the ghosts took control of the hospital and more paranormal occurrences took place, many of which were witnessed. Many people will tell you different haunting accounts in regard to the old Christian Church Hospital.

This was not a place to visit. Mostly boarded up, it had the creepy appearance of something sobering, scary, cold, surreal, and dead. To stare at it too long was to induce a personal feeling of dread and unease. It was partially in use in recent years as an alcoholic treatment center.

Old vintage postcard of Christian Church Hospital.

Although much of the building was heavily boarded, and exits and entrances no longer existed, there were ways a person could gain entry into this deteriorating building and sneak inside. But to say Christian Church Hospital is haunted is an understatement. It's reputed that even drifters and the homeless would not linger near this old structure.

This creepy old hospital is a place where you can **FEEL** its pain and anger—and loneliness. Heaven help those who would tear it down and haul its haunted parts away and rebuild on the same site. Heaven is the only one that can, to borrow a proverbial saying!

There is also a tangible touch of pain about this place. If you stare at it long enough, that pain will make its presence known to you. Shadow figures are often seen in the windows and around the grounds. Orbs are in abundance, and you should be able to capture them on film. The three-windowed roof on the top floor is said to be a showcase for ghost sightings. There are reports of ghosts staring down at living people from these three windows, and elderly people have been seen walking on the rooftop near the edges.

The ghost of a young man standing with the help of wooden crutches has been seen inside a basement window. The ghost of a naked man is seen in another basement window, and he appears to be on his back, dead with eyes fixed and staring at the ceiling. The ghosts of a middle-aged mother with her teenage daughter have been seen at the entrance steps staring up at the door; they are dressed in 1940s clothing. The ghost of an elderly nurse is staring out the fourth floor window; she appears to be crying. The ghost of an older man in a doctor's white coat was seen looking out the window on the second floor. The ghosts of two young nurses staring out a third floor window were once seen; they appeared to be happy and talking together. A gray-haired doctor is seen embracing and kissing a young nurse in her twenties. Those are some of the ghosts seen. There are probably many more yet to reveal themselves to the living.

I would suggest you look at this place and take your photographs from a good, safe distance, and when you begin to sense something watching you or approaching you, move away quickly from that haunted place immediately.

Ghost hunters would probably find more in this hospital than they bargained for...**IF** they attempted to investigate the hauntings. Christian Church Hospital is owned by the city of Kansas. After you visit this uneasy place, go find a nice, quiet restaurant and have a good, nourishing meal and try not to dwell on what you saw there...or *thought* you saw there.

In May 2006, the building was reopened as a compact living community for senior citizens. At this point in time, there have been no new reports of hauntings, paranormal activity, or ghosts lurking in rooms, bathrooms, or hallways. As has often been written about in many paranormal studies involving ghosts and hauntings, the quickest way to awaken ghosts from their sleep (if such a word can be used!) is to tear down the buildings they were living in or by the act of renovating the buildings they once called home! Time will tell.

Other Ghostly Hotspots...

Crown Center

Crown Center is a wonderful, lively complex and a full day can be spent here at leisure. It's located at 2450 Grand Boulevard. With over eighty-five shops, restaurants, and theaters, there is something for everyone to do here! It is also the home for two of Kansas City's largest hotels, the Hyatt Regency Crown Center and the Westin Crown Center.

The famous Hallmark Visitors Center is here as is the Ice Terrace. Given its immense size and comfortable surroundings, it is a favorite place to visit.

Shadow figures have been seen in some public restroom areas. There are reputed to be visits by friendly spirits that mix and blend in with the large crowds and and then vanish as quickly as they materialize.

Elwood Cemetery

Located at Truman and Elwood Streets, this is an easy cemetery to access and visit. It will surprise you with its large array of monuments. For a final resting place, this cemetery had a lot to offer, and it did, to all who lay buried within its comfortable grounds.

If you like gargoyles, you will find them here too. Both sides of the American Civil War are represented here; soldiers from both the North and the South are interned on these grounds. Different wars have their dead here.

Orbs are seen in abundance in this cemetery, day or night. Shadow figures are present, and sometimes not all fade or vanish at human approach, but simply walk away.

For just a walk through some Kansas City history, this is an ideal place to do that — you won't be disappointed. Some people have heard voices behind or near them, but upon turning in the direction of the sound, saw nobody there.

Walking through Elwood Cemetery is like walking through an active landmine of spirits. There is a lot of paranormal activity happening here and much of it is just lurking slightly beyond human vision!

Elwood Cemetery is a cemetery in which you can feel the presence of spirits. These spirits are extremely active and may wish to contact you. You will know when they approach you because their invisible contact may come in the form of touching the end of your nose, ear, face, or your hand. Keep an eye open for the Confederate soldier carrying two rifles in the east section of the cemetery.

Penn Valley Park

Penn Valley Park is found at 31st and Main Streets, across from Crown Center and within walking distance of Union Station. It's a quiet, scenic park—and reputed to have shadow figures on the grounds. Some solid male and female ghosts have also made an appearance. The ghosts of an elderly couple have been seen to appear and then fade into nothingness at sunset.

Swope Park

Swope Park has approximately 1,763 acres and is a scenic beauty spot. It is reputed to have a haunted lake where odd things have been seen in the water and along the shoreline.

Shadow figures have been seen in the picnic areas. The amphitheater is reputed to be haunted by a young man dressed in 1960s clothing.

Union Cemetery

Kansas City is a lively place and there is something for everybody in this old city. A visit to Union Cemetery is a must for people interested in the paranormal.

Located at 227 East 28th Terrace, this cemetery will intrigue you from the moment you arrive until the moment you leave. According to records, Union Cemetery was the first recognized public cemetery in Kansas City.

This cemetery is large, but you can walk it in a full day, becoming involved with reading the grave markers of those interned below your feet. There are over 55,000 graves in this cemetery.

There are soldiers from the American Civil War buried here—and there are stories of their ghosts being seen. Seven Union soldiers in military uniform were seen visiting together, talking, and their lips moving and laughing in silence. Upon approach, two of the soldiers stopped talking and looked directly at the living visitors watching them. Then...*the soldiers vanish*. This has happened before.

An elderly couple, dressed in 1930s clothing, is seen walking together in the western section of the cemetery. They seem oblivious to their surroundings. It is as if they are out for a stroll, enjoying each other's company, and smiling.

One thing you will notice about this cemetery if visiting it with friends or a group at night is the abundance of orbs. There are also an abundance of shadow figures that hover just out of range and fade away upon approach. Is this cemetery haunted? Yes, it is.

Like some cemeteries where there are paranormal occurrences, there are areas where mists form. It's not unusual to see a mist form around a certain grave, or perhaps, two graves. Some mists form over several graves and linger there, as if in communication, or in a form of silent communion with each other.

Sounds of music have been heard in this cemetery. If you listen carefully, you will discover that it comes from an invisible ghost band with a lead trumpeteer. With the 1940s style music playing, tour the cemetery and see who is among the buried. There are famous people buried here and it's fun to discover 'who's who' in the ground.

Other hauntings include hearing the voice of a man singing in French, a child seen running in the south section only to disappear as he turns the corner of a marker, an elderly gentleman dressed in a suit and bowler hat of the Edwardian era, a young woman wearing a blue dress and standing motionless in front of a burial plot, a dog running across the graves who jumps and vanishes in mid-air, a white cat that runs towards the living only to meow and disappear a few feet away, the smell of cinnamon in the air, the smell of cigar smoke, the sound of an owl, an Asian man pointing to the sky and smiling before vanishing into a mist, two ladies dressed in Victorian era clothing leisurely chatting together as they walk arm in arm towards a grave site and vanish at its base, two young sisters playing chase and laughing, and a man dressed in 1880s western clothing with boots and cowboy hat who stares thoughtfully at you and then fades slowly away until there is no trace of him anywhere. These are only a few of the reputed hauntings available to the living visitor who has the time to savor the setting.

You are in for a personal treat if you visit this old cemetery. There is no telling what haunting variations you will encounter. When you have some time, visit Union Cemetery and see what you connect with. You may be very surprised!

Union Station

For the visitor to Kansas City, one of its most interesting historical locations to visit is Union Station. It's located at 30 West Pershing Road. Built in 1914, it encompasses 850,000 square feet and was successfully renovated in 1999.

The Grand Hall contains three, magnificent 3,500 pound chandeliers. Amtrak stops there.

As a cultural location, it also contains fine restaurants and gift shops. The Union Café is found in the Grand Hall under the giant clock, and other eating places include the Harvey House Diner, Pierport's, and the Times Square Concessionaire. If you're looking for a sampling of Kansas City's fine steaks, try the steak dinner at Pierport's located in the northeast corner of Grand Hall. I would recommend the tasty, delicious breakfast omelets available at the Harvey House Diner in the east end of the Grand Hall.

Given its history as a transportation center over the decades, it's no surprise to find hauntings and ghosts. Many incidents of soldier ghosts have occurred, and those are primarily of the World War II type. A World War

Old vintage postcard of Union Station.

I soldier in complete doughboy uniform carrying a rifle over his soldier was reputed to have been a fixture at the entrance of Union Station prior to World War II.

Houston Lake

Located in the Kansas City area, Houston Lake and the Houston Lake Dam are considered haunted. The beach area is reputed to have strange laughter, shadow figures, figures of running children that appear and vanish, a shotgun being fired, and a crying ghost woman who walks the beach area near the dam. The late afternoon through the twilight hours of early evening are when the most macabre things are heard and seen.

Houston Lake is near the Northmoor, Green Acres, and Riverside area within Kansas City. It can be reached by Highway 635, and also via Highways 71 and 29.

17

Haunted Noel, Missouri

Old vintage postcard of Noel, Missouri.

Noel is next to the Elk River, and the town is the location for Bluff Dweller's Cave and Browning Museum. Those visiting the town of Noel will find it a pleasant place, and the tasty breakfasts are typically old-fashioned Missouri meals that please!

Movie Star Ghosts?

There is a story told that the cast of the 1939 classic western, "Jesse James," still hangs out in Noel, Missouri. The cast of the film was housed in Noel during the filming of the movie and included Tyrone Power, Henry Fonda, Nancy Kelly, Randolph Scott, John Carradine, Henry Hull, and Lon Chaney, Jr.

The history of the movie filming was well-documented as was the housing of the cast in this small Missouri town. Whether the appearance of the movie crew resulted in a strong imprint in the ethers and a resulting sporadic residual haunting, so to speak, is anyone's guess.

Bluff Dwellers Cave

Bluff Dwellers Cave is located two miles south of Noel on Highway 59. Like most well-known caves that are open to the public, this cave has a tour schedule. It also has the Browning Museum that houses American Indian artifacts.

Within the cave is a two hundred foot shallow lake. The entire cave is not open to public view or tour.

Human bones, arrows, and various stone implements have been discovered in an ongoing exploration of the cave's interior. Shadow figures have been seen at the cave entrance and inside the cave. There is the story of an American Indian dressed in Indian clothing from the 1800s standing watch at the cave. On approach, this ghost disappears. It's also not seen that often.

The Paranormal activity at Noel, Missouri includes two haunted houses. Noel is a charming, pleasant place, well worth visiting and seeing its unusual bluffs.

The woods seem to have invisible eyes in them watching you, was my impression. I was not alarmed by the sensation of watching eyes and readily accepted it as part of the area's history. I have been in other places where the feeling of being watched was present. I have felt this often in locations where there are mines or caves, and the woods surrounding them.

I suspect that some of this feeling is actually the work of shadow figures going about their business in the daylight hours. Shadow figures are the watchers, watchers anywhere at anytime or any place. As long as there is the living and the dead, there will be the watchers in the woods nearby. My inquisitive nature hopes to find a definite answer to that some day, and explain the why of it!

18

Ghosts are Everywhere

St. Robert, Missouri

St. Robert, Missouri is located in Pulaski County. It is the home of the United States Army training post at Fort Leonard Wood, Missouri. There are stories of ghost soldiers who appear and then fade into shadow figures and vanish. An older soldier is seen as if talking to another person, but there is nobody there, and upon approach, neither is he!

There are many variations of ghost stories found around such military posts throughout the world. With contemporary times comes the appearance of women soldiers, but no women soldier ghosts have been seen at this time in connection with Fort Leonard Wood or St. Robert.

Founded in the early months of World War II, Fort Leonard Wood is a major training base for American soldiers and is one of the more interesting American military bases still in operational use.

It has its share of hauntings, none of which will be commented on by the military. It would be interesting to learn what paranormal occurrences have taken place at this colorful army base since World War II.

From its earliest days, Fort Leonard Wood was known for its rough, rowdy setting, and being full of energy and gusto. Some of those rowdy ghosts are still there.

Paris, Missouri

Paris, Missouri is not a great distance from Hannibal. Some of its first settlers arrived in 1818 and by 1831 it was establishing itself as a strong community. Located in Monroe County near the middle fork area of Salt River, it is a pleasant, small town where you can have a good cup of coffee with apple pie while visiting with people.

Mark Twain was born not far from here, and other notable people in the arts include artist Gordon Snidow and writer Mary Margaret McBride. The Mark Twain Lake is not far from the town.

This is an unusual town with its old train depot and tracks area, the covered bridge found due west of the town, the old courthouse, and Founders Cemetery. Just walking in the area gives you a feel for Missouri's history.

Founders Cemetery is reputed to have orbs at night. To walk through this charming cemetery is a study in old Missouri grave markings.

The old depot train area is reputed to be haunted by the ghosts of railroad men from the late 1800s, and the upper floors of the old courthouse are also reputed to be haunted.

Paris is a charming town, a solid piece of Americana still intact, and a trip to the bridge is a delight. Some of the best apple pie with steaming hot black coffee to be found anywhere is found in the town of Paris, Missouri!

Shelbina, Missouri

Shelbina, Missouri is located on Highways 36 and 15, and was nicknamed in the late 1800s as the "Queen City of the Prairie." Noted for its Southern customs, it was founded in 1857. Its unique social history includes such organizations as the Red Hats Society, Old Threshers, Sons of Confederacy, Odd Fellows Lodge, Shelbina Masonic Lodge, American Legion, Eastern Star, and the Women's Auxiliary. It's also home to several churches.

There are two cemeteries there, St. Mary's Catholic Cemetery and Shelbina Cemetery; both are old and in use. These two cemeteries are reputed to have orbs and ghost sightings.

For a nice, filling steak dinner, you may want to visit the Front Row restaurant, which is located at 109 South Center next to the Shelbina Historical Society and across from the Shelbina Public Library. This restaurant offers delicious steak dinners you will savor and remember long after the meal is finished!

The town has amenities and places to eat, and is nice to stroll through. This town is a pleasant stop whatever your destination. Check out the beautiful Shelbina Lake, established in 1937, while you're in the town.

Mexico, Missouri

Mexico, Missouri is an old Missouri city with a colorful past. Mexico was incorporated as a town in 1855 and its *The Mexico Ledger* is one of Missouri's oldest newspapers still publishing. The city is reputed to have several paranormal areas that include Hardin Park, Robert S. Green Park, and the Presser Performing Arts Center. In addition to excellent bluegrass music, the ghost hunter can also visit surrounding area cemeteries and look for orbs!

Hardin Park is located at South Clark and Clay Streets. It has a haunted bandstand area called the Leach Gazebo, in which shadow figures have been seen. Many summer concerts are enjoyed at this park.

The Robert S. Green Park, located at Muldrow and Hisey Streets, contains two museums and a gazebo. Shadow figures appear at different times near the gazebo and the Audrain County Historical Museum located within the park. A Confederate soldier is said to be seen sometimes at twilight.

The Presser Performing Arts Center, built in 1925, is reputed to have voices, whispers, and the ghost of a young woman who appears in the balcony and vanishes as quickly as she appears. The ghost of a child was once seen running across the stage...only to vanish before the little boy reached the other side.

This pleasant, small Missouri city is certainly an intriguing place to visit and tour. Any visitor who comes to this city will enjoy a nice stroll through its historic downtown and a view of its buildings.

St. James, Missouri

Settled in the early 1800s, St. James started its existence as a trading post in one of the most heavily wooded areas of Missouri. The Meramec Spring Park is located here and has one of the largest springs in Missouri.

There are an abundance of good places to eat in this town, and you may wish to sample the excellent pasta at Sybill's. Ferrigno Winery, Heinrichshaus, Meramec Vineyards, and St. James Winery are here and are noted for their fine wine production. If you have time for lunch, give the Bistro d'Vine a try when you visit St. James Winery.

Meramec Springs Park is noted for its shadow figures. The Missouri Veterans Home and Cemetery is noted for paranormal activity including shadow figures, and ghosts in the cemetery. World War II ghost soldiers have been seen, but they fade and disappear when approached by the living. Frequent residual hauntings are reputed to occur in the cemetery.

Salem, Missouri

First settled in 1829 with several families, Salem is an interesting historical city that also served as a skirmish point between Union and Confederate soldiers in late 1861. The Confederates lost this battle to the Union and this was one of the first, early victories for the Union during the American Civil war.

The city has many churches and organizations for its size, and the Dent County Courthouse is one of the Victorian era architectural highlights. The courthouse was built in 1871.

The Dent County Courthouse is reputed to have a male ghost in the attic, and he haunts the top floor in the early evening hours after sunset. North Lawn Cemetery and the Salem Cedar Grove Cemetery are reputed to have paranormal activity. Shadow figures have been seen at both cemeteries, with American Civil War soldier ghosts appearing at Salem Cedar Grove.

Salem is an interesting city and a place where you can find an excellent cup of coffee with fresh coconut cream pie and friendly conversation. For a journey into a town with a colorful historical past, you will find this an enjoyable city to visit.

Licking, Missouri

Settlers established Licking, Missouri in 1826. During the American Civil War there was massive destruction and the city was forced to rebuild.

A town with a colorful history, it was also the home of actress Miyoshi Umeki (1929–2007). Born in Otaru, Japan, she died in Licking at age 78. Umeki was a gifted actress and singer, best remembered for her Oscar winning role for Best Supporting Actress in the popular movie, "Sayonara" (1957), in which she played the role of Katsumi and co-starred with actors Red Buttons and Marlon Brando.

There were many deaths in the city, but one involving the murder of a family aroused the wrath of the community. Jody Hamilton was hung in late 1906 for the cruel murder of the Parsons family, and the ghost of a crying man is said to be seen near the hanging site on courthouse property. Is this the repentant ghost of Hamilton, or another ghost of a different person?

In 1905 the original Collier Hotel burned down, resulting in the death of three people. The ghosts of these three people are reputed to haunt the immediate area of their deaths.

There are also ghost hauntings and orbs at Boone Creek Cemetery. This well-kept cemetery is approximately four miles south of Licking near Boone Creek Baptist Church; the church owns and maintains this nineteenth century cemetery that is still in use.

Cabool, Missouri

Cabool, Missouri is approximately sixty-six miles from Springfield and located near the Mark Twain National Forest in Texas County. The town was settled in the 1800s.

Within Cabool's radius are six cemeteries that bear closer examination by those who are interested in paranormal activity and ghosts. Shadow figures and ghosts have been seen. Orbs are in abundance. If you are in this immediate area, visit the following cemeteries: Atis, Cabool, Cedar Bluff, Hamilton, Macedonia, and Sargent. You will find some interesting paranormal happenings.

West Plains, Missouri

The historic downtown of West Plains was established in 1885. It is a nice town to visit, and to enjoy a cup of hot coffee with a cinnamon roll.

It is close to several cemeteries, including Spears Graveyard, Oaklawn, Hall, and Howell County cemeteries. Each cemetery has some elements of paranormal activity. Spears Cemetery had three shadow figures.

Visit the nearby Rockbridge Mill while you're in this area. Although no longer functioning as a working mill, it has great historical value and is interesting to observe; it was built in 1841 and then intense fighting during the Civil War destroyed the beautiful area. In 1868, a rebuilding process started, and today Rockbridge Mill is noted for Rainbow trout fishing and its fine restaurant.

Mountain Grove, Missouri

Mountain Grove is blessed with an interesting and beautiful location in Missouri, and is also the site of the Aid-Hodgson Mill, Faurot Hall, and the Mountain Grove Square and Bandstand. The square's bandstand was originally built in 1915, and like the square itself, is listed on the National Register of Historic Places. The Aid-Hodgson Mill is an extremely atmospheric scene, filled with a sense of nostalgia. It's a setting that is inclined to induce feelings of solitude. I have visited places looking for paranormal activity, ghosts, and hauntings, and rarely am I distracted by any particular structure than the one I am searching for to investigate. This old mill did distract me with its innate beauty and sense of defined time and space. If you are in Mountain Grove, take the opportunity to visit this old mill. You won't be disappointed with its enduring structure and charm.

Within driving distance of the city are over twenty-five cemeteries, and it will take some time to reach them all, but if you persevere, you will find some haunted cemeteries to your liking. There are probably more than twenty-five in this area, but here are some that have had reputed hauntings, orbs, and paranormal activity over the decades: Swede Cemetery, Frog Knob Cemetery, Absher Cemetery, Clinton Cemetery, Willow Springs Cemetery, Helum Cemetery, Mountain Valley Cemetery, Macedonia Cemetery, Canada Cemetery, Strunk Cemetery, Lone Star Cemetery, and Stubbs Cemetery.

Thayer, Missouri

Thayer is in Oregon County and was established as a prosperous railroad town in 1882. The cemetery had some presences, and a few shadow figures that were evasive and then vanished.

For an excellent meal, and somewhere to remember for its friendly atmosphere, there is a place called Warm Fork Restaurant at 210 Risner Street. Good steak, good coffee, and good service, coupled with many friendly people, made this an enjoyable visit.

Cemeteries in this county are not difficult to find, and if you become lost searching for them, get directions from the local people. Other cemeteries with paranormal activity include Myrtle, Cave Springs, Garfield, Cotton Creek, Liberty, and New Salem.

Doniphan, Missouri

Doniphan is located in Ripley County and its history dates back to the early 1800s. Here you will find the following cemeteries: Martin, Antioch, Cyclone, and Amity. There have been some paranormal activity reported in the cemeteries. Ripley County also has its share of shadow figures.

Poplar Bluff, Missouri

Nicknamed the "Gateway to the Ozarks," Poplar Bluff is a comfortable city nestled close along the Black River. Originally a railroad town, it was also a source for lumber.

Black River was important for shipping. Another aspect was the river's usefulness as a steamboat-building site. In the early 1800s American Indians settled the area; Solomon Kittrell was among the early settlers in 1819.

There is a lovely, well-kept pet cemetery at 195 Mallard Trail called Precious Acres Pet Cemetery; it's a restful and peaceful place. If you have the time, stop by and see its pleasant pet burial grounds.

Poplar Bluff Cemetery is located at 1901 North Main Street and has paranormal activity. There are several shadow figures and the ghost of a young man in his twenties wearing coveralls walks the western section. He is looking at the ground as if he is searching for something he dropped, lost, or possibly misplaced. He is a residual haunting that seems to linger longer than most.

Memorial Gardens Cemetery, at 3556 South Westwood Boulevard, had a sense of presences, but nothing specific.

Within driving range of the city are many cemeteries. If you have time, it would be an interesting side trip for you to find them and see what paranormal occurences you discover within each! Ask the local people for directions.

Carthage, Missouri

Located in Jasper County, Carthage is oftentimes called the Maple Leaf Tree City due to its beautiful abundance of maple trees. Founded in 1841, its oldest area is the site of the original courthouse and Carthage Square.

During the American Civil War there was much fighting for control of this city, which the Confederacy won after a bloody battle on July 5, 1861; the battle became known historically as the first Battle of Carthage; this was followed by the second bloody battle of Carthage in 1863 in which the Union won control of the city.

Carthage residents were split over the question of slavery and whether the North or the South would have its total loyalty. Both the North and South considered the area a much sought after prize. The town was destroyed and burned in 1864 by Confederate guerilla forces.

With the resurgence of the railroad, nearby lead mines, and limestone quarries, the town made an immediate comeback after the war, and many Victorian houses were built. The American Civil War Museum is located at 205 Grant Street.

Ghost stories and hauntings abound in this pleasant city, and cemeteries in the county are reputed to have cold spots. The Carthage Courthouse is said to be haunted by the ghost of a woman on the second floor, and two male ghosts also inhabit the courthouse. One male ghost haunts the attic while the other male ghost haunts the basement. Other paranormal activity has been noted in the Carthage Square area and in various Victorian houses. Shadow figures are frequently seen in the city and around old houses. The locations of the lead mines and limestone quarries are believed to be haunted by Confederate soldier ghosts. Union soldier ghosts have been seen in the woods and outlying countryside.

An intriguing, friendly city, it's one you will enjoy visiting and savoring its special spectral atmosphere.

Stone County, Missouri

Stone County is a location that has numerous small cemeteries, many of which are now forgotten or inactive. Have a cup of coffee and apple pie at the excellent Crane Café, 206 West Main Street, in Crane, and start from there.

Crane is but one of the many small towns in Stone County; others include Galena and Reeds Springs. Get an early start, and plan a day checking out these small cemeteries. Some will have shadow figures while others have a paranormal feeling about them.

No residual hauntings have been encountered, but presences exist. You will find this an enjoyable journey with some surprises along the way!

Nevada, Missouri

Nevada, Missouri, located in Vernon County, has an interesting history. Some of its notable natives include Senator Eva Bowring of Nebraska, Director/actor John Huston, and outlaw Frank James, who was the brother of Jesse James. It's approximately a one-hour drive north of the city of Joplin. Once inhabited by the Osage Indians as its homeland, it became opened to settlement with the help of these Indians in 1821.

The time leading up to and including the American Civil War saw this area as primarily pro-South, and men from the region fought with the Confederates in the bloody encounter known as the Battle of Wilson's Creek at Springfield, Missouri. The city of Nevada had its own Lady Bushwhackers, who spied for the Confederacy, including Ella Mayfield. After the war, the town rebuilt and tended to its wounds, once again becoming a prosperous community. The new town was functioning by 1867.

In the 1880s, the Lunatic Asylum State Hospital No. 3 was established. For those seeking to learn about paranormal occurrences, patient ghosts, and hauntings, this location is aptly inhabited by such phenomena. Repeated hauntings by ghosts from the American Civil War era have been seen in older parts of the city, and the county's cemeteries have also had sightings of ghosts. This is a pleasant town, and people will visit with you. A good meal is to be had here. This is an entertaining place for any ghost hunter to visit for a day!

Warrensburg, Missouri

Located in Johnson County, the city was established in 1871 and the University of Central Missouri is located here. The Missouri Pacific train wreck in 1904 resulted in thirty people being killed—their ghosts are said to haunt the place of their death and the downtown.

There are two cemeteries in the city, Warrensburg Cemetery Association and Memorial Gardens. Both cemeteries have orbs and shadow figures.

The University of Central Missouri is reputed to have ghost hauntings. One of these ghosts is a former teacher, Laura J. Yeater, who haunts the building named after her. The second ghost is that of a male janitor who haunts the administration building.

Part Eighteen: Ghosts are Everywhere

Knob Noster, Missouri

Knob Noster was established in 1850. Knob Noster State Park and Whiteman Air Force Base are part of this quiet community. A mile north of the current location of the city is where the original town was built. The original town burned and is now said to be the site of reputed shadow figures.

Sedalia, Missouri

Sedalia is noted for many interesting happenings. It had its origins as a railroad town in 1860 and during the American Civil War was a Union military post in place to protect the railroad system. It remained a Union post until the post closed in 1865.

What remains of the railroad era is best seen at Katy Depot; built in 1896 and renovated in 2001 to become the site for the Chamber of Commerce, Katy Depot is located at 600 East Third Street. Walking through this city is a rewarding experience. There is a distinct sense of history and the old buildings reflect that gracefulness from the past.

This is the place where Scott Joplin and his world-famous ragtime music got underway and influenced American jazz music with its complexity and innovative sound. The Scott Joplin Foundation is located here.

There are three public parks reputed to have shadow figures: Hubbard, Vermont, and Housel. A thriving city of over 20,000 people, there are places to eat and visit. Crown Hill Cemetery is said to have American Civil War ghosts from both the North and the South.

Boonville, Missouri

There are over four hundred properties in Boonville, Missouri listed on the National Register of Historic Places. Established in 1805 as a salt mining area, the city had its start with the Hannah Cole family homestead in 1810.

The site of several American Civil War skirmishes and battles, the city held its own and survived the war. There are many ghosts in Boonville!

Although it has been replaced, the original Boonville Bridge built in 1924 has numerous reputed hauntings. The Cooper County Courthouse, originally built in 1823, was rebuilt again in 1912 and is said to have the ghost of a lawyer haunting its third floor. In 1848 the Hanging Barn and jail were constructed with the last hanging documented in 1930. Ghost sightings are prevalent at these locations.

It's widely believed that the Forest Hill house is haunted with the ghost of Thomas W. Nelson. This restored house is also known as the Thomas W. Nelson Home and is located at 700 10th Street. Nelson's ghost is said to appear in the early evening, standing on the balcony of the second gallery, staring out across the lawn.

The Ballentine House built in 1828 contains the ghost of a young woman who's seen standing at the front entrance door. Who she is or what era she's from is unknown.

Other hauntings and ghosts have been seen on the second floor and in the third floor ballroom of the Roslyn Heights house built in 1895. It's located at 821 Main Street.

Two cemeteries are known haunted spots with shadow figures and ghosts of American Civil War soldiers. They are Sunset Hill Cemetery, established in 1835, and Walnut Grove Cemetery, established in 1852. An abundance of orbs has also been reported at both cemeteries.

There are over thirty cemeteries in Cooper County near Boonville. Each cemetery may contain haunting variations, paranormal activity, orbs, and ghosts; they are there for the interested ghost hunter. Be sure you have your camera with you when you visit them!

Fayette, Missouri

Fayette, Missouri is a heavily wooded, scenic town located approximately thirteen miles from Boonville. Located in Howard County, the year 1810 marked the arrival of the first permanent settlers in a location previously settled by American Indians. The town was named for the Frenchman, Marquis de Lafayette.

Something that will definitely intrigue ghost hunters is that there are over thirty cemeteries in the county, and each may contain paranormal surprises waiting to be discovered! Some of these cemeteries may have Union and Southern soldier ghosts. Be sure to have a camera on hand should you visit any of these old cemeteries.

There is also the Courthouse Tower that is said to be haunted, along with the gazebo and the courthouse building.

The main street has arts, shops, and restaurants. Smiley Library and Central Methodist University are located in this prosperous city that has over twelve churches. If you have time, you may wish to visit Stephens Museum at Central Methodist University.

Fayette was settled by Southerners, and this area of Missouri is often referred to as the Little Dixie Region. You will find many fascinating things about this old Missouri city.

Moberly, Missouri

Moberly is an interesting old railroad town in Randolph County. As it seemed to appear whole overnight, according to legend, it was nicknamed "The Magic City." The town is known affectionately as Little Dixie and was originally settled by Southerners beginning in 1829; the city was founded in 1866.

There is much to see in this colorful town, including a visit to the Little Dixie Regional Library at 111 North Fourth Street and Moberly's Antique Mall. If you become enchanted with this town as most do, you may want to read about its history in the well-written, three-volume set of books titled *History of Moberly 1865 through 1896* by Ralph Gerhard, which is available from the Chamber of Commerce.

If you're hungry, there are restaurants available. The town is clean and neat in its well-maintained appearance.

The site of the original Wabash Depot is reputed to be haunted by the ghosts of children, and some of the old buildings are said to have paranormal activity with residual hauntings.

The five cemeteries within Randolph County should not be overlooked. They are each close to Moberly and within a short driving distance. Moberly is a friendly town, and its excellent coffee is perfect for drinking!

St. Joseph, Missouri

The history of St. Joseph, Missouri begins with the establishment of fur trading routes and the business foresight of Joseph Robidoux in the year 1790. It was named in 1834 and was well established as a city by 1860.

One of Missouri's most haunted cities, it has long been a favorite in the state for ghost hunters. There are many accounts of the walking dead witnessed in various old homes; a loved one or past inhabitant who appears, walks about as if on a journey somewhere, and then vanishes. For an in depth look at various hauntings, there is plenty of food for thought in the local library archives and in the newspaper historical files.

Many houses in this city are said to be haunted—and many have a *PERMANENT* ghost guest! Sometimes, there is more than one ghost. For those interested in finding a gaggle of ghosts in one city, this would be an ideal place to spend some time.

Lake Pomme de Terre, Missouri

Lake Pomme de Terre is located in Hickory County. The area's history dates back to the 1840s. Many small towns are in the area. The lake is reputed to have bobbing heads, and its shoreline reputed to have shadow figures. Hickory County is heavily wooded and blessed with a beautiful array of colorful scenery.

Possum Trot, Missouri

Possum Trot was once a town in Stone County, Missouri. It has been forgotten with the passage of time and demolished by the elements. Nature has reclaimed it completely. All that remains of this town is found in the abandoned ruins of a church and house. Its life, its history, its hopes, fears, dreams, and its people have gone elsewhere.

There is a sense of solitude about the area, and the church has shadow figures. If you are driving, its approximate location is eight miles southwest of Nixa, Missouri on what is identified as Missouri Route M; there is much beautiful scenery to take in.

I came across a very old, rusted horseshoe at the church, which had been partially buried under scattered bricks. The day was beautiful, clear, and had a warm breeze when my wife Debra and I visited the remains of this ghost town. We found a strange door ajar, almost like a *PORTAL* asking to be entered...which we did not.

On the front of the door were three shadow figures that shaped themselves into what could best be described as an outstretched three-fingered claw, depending on your personal interpretation. It was something once seen you did not easily forget. What message the shadows were trying to communicate we did not know. There were no clues as to what was trying to be expressed to the world of the living by the world of the paranormal.

Upon returning to the door five minutes later, the shadows were gone. I cannot explain this, nor will I hazard a guess. Those interested will have to look it over for themselves and see what they see!

While examining one of the structures, I walked around towards the rear of it. Debra saw two young boys exit the other side and come around in the opposite direction since they had seen me. These two ghosts vanished when they saw Debra observing them. Debra said the ghost boys looked totally surprised that she had seen them and there was a look of curiosity on their faces as they vanished into thin air! It was a delightful trip!

Part Eighteen: Ghosts are Everywhere

Possum Trot, Missouri.

Bolivar, Missouri

Bolivar, Missouri is located on Highway 13. There are stories of both Union and Confederate ghosts that still walk the area roads. An older man dressed in Confederate clothes and cap walks a back road to Bolivar, carrying a white, stuffed bag. On approach, he vanishes. There is a look of pain in his face.

Two Union soldiers on foot have been seen walking on a road west of the town. They also vanish when approached. They seem to be laughing together about something.

19

The Dead and Beyond

Uneasy Spirits of Woodlock Cemetery
Davisville, Missouri

Located in Crawford County on a hilltop, this old cemetery of Davisville, Missouri is the talk of many a ghost hunter who has been there, studied the surroundings, and come away satisfied that there is paranormal activity in the cemetery in the form of shadow figures.

Voices without bodies have been heard. A woman crying but not seen has been heard at different times.

The sound of an object being struck repeatedly by an ax has been heard on hot, windy days. A growling cat is heard, but never seen.

The Walking Dead of Wheeler Cemetery
Dixon, Missouri

Wheeler Cemetery is noted for its paranormal activity. Dixon is an old Missouri town that got its start as a prosperous Frisco Railroad location in 1869. Located in Pulaski County, it retains the charm of small town Missouri with amenities.

Wheeler Cemetery has haunting stories going back in time to the late 1800s. There's a story about two fighting, drunk railroad men at the cemetery edge, who enter the cemetery and vanish.

Voices have frequently been heard. The laughter from a group of children at play has been heard on Saturdays. Being touched by something invisible is not uncommon.

Ghosts in the Morgue
Mount Vernon, Missouri

Mount Vernon is noted for its stone courthouse built in 1901. This remarkable architectural structure has a ghost haunting its basement. The city has an annual Apple Butter Makin' Days celebration, and eight miles away is the annual celebration of German heritage at the Ernte Fest of Freistatt, Missouri. Located in Lawrence County, Mount Vernon's courthouse is on the National Register of Historic Places. But most important of all to those interested in the paranormal, Mount Vernon has a haunted building filled with shadow figures and ghosts. This building is now the Missouri Rehab Center, but in the past it was known as the Chest Hospital for Tuberculosis Patients and at one time included the Veteran's Home. It's located at 600 North Main Street. The old, original section had three floors and a haunted attic. Ghosts of people wearing hospital nightgowns have frequently been seen.

There are reputed ghosts everywhere. Not surprising, there are many ghosts of former hospital patients wandering about. Much paranormal activity centralized in the older part of the building occurs with frequency. The ghosts of many patients who died in the hospital are still there and active. There are both residual and intelligent hauntings.

Scenes of the walking dead have taken place where a ghost or ghosts have moved through closed hallway doors. Ghosts will appear at certain doors in the hospital, but on closer examination the rooms were found to be empty. Unexplained sounds and voices have been heard. Names of unknown persons have been called out in otherwise empty corridors. There are many cold spots, and strange breezes when the windows are closed and the air and heating system is turned off. Being touched by invisible people has been said to take place in different areas of the hospital where many patients have died. A full paranormal investigation of this old structure would be most interesting to undertake...if such an investigation could take place.

Widespread rumors of paranormal occurrences in the old hospital's basement are still prevalent, and have become part of the hospital's history. Many people have come away from this building aware that something more than the ordinary lurks there, **SOMETHING** tangible and active. It's reputed that people who work at the hospital do not go into the basement alone at night. Why are there so many macabre and strange occurrences taking place in the basement? The answer is simple. Located in the basement is the original haunted morgue.

Deadman's Pond
Reeds Springs, Missouri

An interesting place to visit, Reeds Springs is not far from Springfield, Missouri. There is a pond near the town that was the scene of a bloody battle during the American Civil War between the local guard and guerrilla bands made up of bushwhackers and outlaws. Legend has it that over a hundred guerrilla members were massacred near this pond situated between the small towns of Galena and Reeds Spring, Missouri. Some bodies were left to rot in the woods and many other bodies were dumped into the pond to sink, fester, rot, decay, and vanish within the mud and water. Today, stories of orbs, mist figures, and shadow figures are said to haunt the pond area, and vanish upon approach. Bones have been found in the pond.

The sound of a man calling the name of "Susan" near this area has been heard, but the ghost has never been seen. Only the lonely, sad voice has been heard....

Galena and Reeds Springs are only a little over eight miles from each other by way of Highway 413. Driving this route, stopping to examine an area here and there, proved to be a lively adventure. I saw a roan horse stroll across the highway in front of my car, turn its beautiful face towards me, and then watched as it disappeared halfway across the highway.

It's my opinion that this quiet, unassuming stretch of highway is haunted. I did not have a lot of time to explore the area in detail, but I saw what I saw, and the feelings of other presences were apparent to me on this stretch of highway. There may be other things lurking in those woods not yet revealed or discovered!

I asked myself: What might lie buried under the highway that travels it freely in ghostly fashion? Did one or more bushwhackers or guardsmen die along the highway route to forever haunt the area seeking solace or safety?

Travel this highway and see it for yourself. Allow this beautiful land to touch you with its presences. See what you encounter.

I suggest a night and a day trip for comparison. I found each had its own sense of hauntings. Perhaps, take a friend who's also interested in the paranormal with you and compare notes. But be careful if you go alone at night. I have found that there really are things that go bump in the night, and in the day, too....

Cemetery Screamers
Windyville, Missouri

Windyville, Missouri is located not far from Cedar Ridge, and is the site of reputed hauntings. Its haunted history is well-known from many sources. The location at the old tomato canning factory is considered haunted, and there have been sightings of shadow figures and orbs near and within the structure. Some empty structures have been called haunted for various reasons.

There is a cemetery within two miles of the town that has been the location for macabre hauntings involving unseen persons, whose screams vanish as quickly as they are heard. There are no signs of humans casting the terrifying screams...only the empty and eerie atmosphere of Lone Rock Cemetery near Indian Creek.

Aurora Camp is located here. The School of Metaphysics campus is located at 163 Moon Valley Road and has an online computer site that includes a dream school and dream analysis. Many of the structures in this town are empty, but it's not a ghost town as there are living residents.

As to the paranormal, I encountered nothing out of the unusual when I visited this section of Missouri in 2008. Following Highway K is a nice drive, and if you feel like pausing on it at times, you will enjoy the nature. Names of small communities such as Plad, Long Lane, Cedar Ridge, and others dot the area.

This is essentially peaceful country, and gives the visitor a sense of nostalgia simply by passing through the area on its various roads. If you enjoy traveling in a peaceful, rural setting, then Dallas County might become for you an enjoyable and pleasant drive.

One of the added charms in this immediate area would be a visit to Bennett Springs State Park, on Highway 64 near Lebanon, Missouri, which gives a grand look at the Ozark Mountains, an area with many superstitions, Indian tales, and happenings of various kinds. There is an old, 1930s restaurant on site, modernized and still in operation. There is camping, fishing, hiking, and a chance to walk the Natural Tunnel Trail, Savanna Ridge Trail, and Stream Trail.

This peaceful park has not changed much since I was there as a child. As a child, I was told by different relatives that a young woman drowned there and her walking, restless ghost is seen near the restaurant when the moonlight is at its brightest.

20

And Other Ghostly Tales...

The Ghost of Alf Bolin, Ozark, Missouri

During the American Civil War, the name of Alf Bolin struck fear into the hearts of Missourians. Born at Spokane, Missouri, Bolin was a vicious bushwhacker and serial killer.

Bolin was a cruel, deranged man who killed at random and his victims included children. He generally tortured his victims before he murdered them. His methods of torture for personal amusement terrified the people in South Missouri, and Bolin's evil legend of cruel tortures and murders spread quickly.

First, he robbed his victims. If it was a woman, she was also raped and mutilated. If it was a man, his testicles were crushed slowly with whatever was at hand including sharp rocks and then he was castrated. Sometimes the male victim was hanged by the testicles, then castrated prior to being murdered. Ripping out the tongues of his victims was another passion greatly enjoyed by Alf Bolin, among many other heinous tortures he devised for each victim. Sometimes, he simply robbed people and let them go on their way, which was not too often.

Bolin's murders were many and went unchecked until a Union soldier killed him on February 2, 1863. This Union soldier killed and decapitated Bolin, impaled Bolin's head on a pole, and afterwards took Bolin's bloody head to Ozark, Missouri for display. The end of this human monster's life and his atrocities was a time of intense celebration by the settlers who lived in the area. There was celebrating, joy, and relief everywhere in Ozark and elsewhere at the news of the Bolin's death. Some danced a circle around his gruesome head, laughed, and spit on the dead man's face.

What became of Alf Bolin's decapitated head has many different endings, but it mysteriously disappeared. Bolin's body was buried without its head somewhere on Swan Cave Road in Chadwick, Missouri.

Murder Rocks, a haunted area with strange cries, eerie wind sounds, night screams, and muffled voices of different women crying out in pain, was one of Bolin's personally selected sites for tortures and numerous murders. Murder Rocks holds the memories of Bolin's torture fantasies carried out in reality, and the land is considered haunted as a result of his evil misdeeds. The area is located a few miles from Branson, Missouri.

A social misfit, Alf Bolin kept the precise location of his secret horde of money stolen from his victims to himself, with the exception of what he shared with his fellow psychotics who made up his outlaw gang of fifteen to twenty-five men. Bolin had a widespread reputation of surrounding himself with men who thought and acted the same way he did.

To this day, his accumulation of money and its hidden location remains a secret, only that it's known to be buried near caves found in Taney County, Missouri. He took that secret to his grave.

Many ghost stories have grown about Alf Bolin's headless body searching for its head on clear, full moon nights in Ozark, Missouri. Even more ghost stories have continued about things seen and heard around Murder Rocks. I was told that Murder Rocks was not a place to visit at night unless you were with a group of people. There have been stories of people visiting the area and swearing they would never return because of what they saw and heard.

Indian Ghost Cave, Cassville, Missouri

Cassville, Missouri is a quiet rural city with an interesting history that started in 1835. A site of importance during the American Civil War, it was a military setting for forces of both the Union and the Confederacy.

In 1861, it was designated the Confederate capitol of Missouri. There are Union and Confederate soldiers buried in Cassville. The city is located seven miles from Roaring River State Park.

There are many caves in the Cassville area, and Cassville is in Barry County. Barry County has caves, some found and open, but many collapsed or their locations forgotten.

Debra and I were told of an old Indian cave in the rural area south of Cassville that had been opened due to a hillslide. This was in 1995, and together, we visited the cave that February.

The woods and small creek gave the area a misty look, and it was frequented by bears at the time of our visit. We both had a feeling of presences. Shadow figures were found in the cave, and it was evident there had been some excavation by amateurs done. The amateurs had dug carelessly, moving rocks and dirt at random without attention to detail. The cave entrance has since been collapsed and filled in by another hillslide.

Cry of the Banshee, Devil's Elbow, Missouri

Located approximately five miles east of St. Robert, Missouri on the Big Piney River, this area is reputed to be haunted by the screams and moans of a woman calling a man's name. The name is never clearly heard.

Sightings of bobbing heads that vanish under the water and do not resurface have been seen on Big Piney River. The winds have unusual sounds carried with them, like wisps of laughter or crying. Strange things have been seen floating just below the surface of the water.

The Ghost of Wyatt Earp Lamar, Missouri

Lamar, Missouri is located in Barton County and is the birthplace of President Harry S. Truman (1884–1972). Another famous resident of Lamar is the western icon, Wyatt Earp (1848–1929).

Wyatt Earp married his first wife, Urilla Sutherland (1849–1870), at Lamar, and they lived together in Lamar until her untimely death during childbirth from typus.

One of the stories is that the ghosts of Wyatt and Urilla Earp are seen walking hand in hand near the area of their first home during the early evening hours.

Another ghost story is that the ghosts of President Harry S. Truman and his wife are seen walking in the city during the early evening hours.

Witch Ghosts

California has the most number of active Witches and Pagans in the United States. Missouri is the second most ranked state. Missouri has its share of ghost stories concerning deceased Witches. As followers of this old religion prefer it, I will spell "Witch" and "Witchcraft" with the capital letter "W." As Christians use a capital letter "C" in discussing and writing about their religion, the same respect and courtesy will be shown to those of different mainstream religions. Much to the Christian dismay, Witchcraft is well on its way to becoming a mainstream religion.

I am not a Witch, or a Wiccan, or a Pagan in the traditional sense, but I do know and have many friends who are. I respect their efforts to endure and remove the distortions leveled upon them by other religions and society.

Gerina Dunwich is a witch and has spent a lifetime correcting misconceptions concerning being a Witch and Witchcraft. I am her friend and admire her for her dedication. There are many others I also know. Another fine writer and Witch who has done much to expose and correct the misconceptions surrounding Witchcraft is Raymond Buckland.

Missouri has been a location for Witchcraft since the 1800s, and although it's still hidden to a great degree, it is very active and very much alive. There are 537 covens in the state of Missouri and fifty-four of them are in the Springfield, Missouri, Greene County area.

Some are public. Some are private. Some members use their real names whereas other members use a coven name to protect their identities from nutcases trying to make life miserable for them. There is a wide range of information about Witchcraft on the Internet, in libraries, and in bookstores that readers should have no difficulty finding what they seek to know about this positive, nature-based religion. Unlike other mainstream religions, Witchcraft does not have a central, organized line of command and authority. In that regard, it could be compared favorably to Hinduism, the great religious system of ancient India. Unlike Christianity and Islam, Hinduism and Witchcraft do not seek to destroy their competition through consolidation or force because they do not seek out new members. Furthermore, Hinduism and Witchcraft practice an honest approach of "live and let live," and do not actively seek recruits or followers.

Whereas some mainstream religions have assigned one-way-only-choice of designated deities such as Jesus Christ, Buddha, and Mohammed, Hinduism and Witchcraft do not. The choices are more open in Hinduism and Witchcraft, and it is the responsibility of each individual to make a personal choice and take responsibility for that choice without threat of coercion.

Essentially, religion is a personal choice and depends on how the individual is shaped by his or her culture, and what personal growth choices are made along the way towards living a meaningful life. For those interested in studying these themes further, the following books are suggested reading: *The Mysteries of Mithras: The Pagan Belief that Shaped the Christian World* by Payam Nabarz, *Christianity: The Origins of a Pagan Religion* by Philippe Walter, *Witchcraft: The Old Religion* by Leo Louis Martello, *Origins of Modern Witchcraft: The Evolution of a World Religion* by Ann Moura, and *The Rebirth of Witchcraft* by Doreen Valiente.

In Missouri, and many other states, sometimes a Witch was mistakenly identified as an Old Herbal Woman, or an Herb Woman, thus escaping being labeled as a Witch. This explains why many people will recall having heard a strange story or tale about someone who was an old herb lady in the rural sector. Missouri is full of tales about the Hill People and their ways of healing and herb use, and in South Missouri, these people were prevalent until the 1950s when the American culture took up an interest in the paranormal, supernatural, and the occult. Now, everybody is a potential herbalist or Witch!

Check your memories. Think about when you were once told about the old woman who lived alone and worked herbs, and you'll begin to see the picture unfold perfectly for you. There are numerous hauntings in Missouri, and the world, in which the Witch is a focal force and character. Sometime, when somebody tells you "that old ruin of a house belonged to a Witch and her ghost haunts the house," remember she was probably just a highly knowledgeable herb woman doing what came natural to her. Had she lived during the cruel Burning Times, the Catholic Church would have branded her (or him!) a Witch, tortured a confession from that poor soul, and confiscated the person's land, money, and holdings. Of course, the United States had its own modified version of the hysteria surrounding Witches with its Salem Witch Trials held in 1692. Witchcraft is not related or akin to Satanism in any shape, form, or way. Satanism relies on a Christian God, a Christian Devil, and a Christian afterlife concept to exist and function by. Witchcraft does not, and never did, since it does not accept the Christian concepts of a Christian God, a Christian Devil, or a Christian afterlife. In the final analysis, to each his or her own choice regarding a personal religion or philosophy to live by! More compassion, understanding, and respect for another person's right to worship would go a long way in healing the ills of this old world. Taken collectively, humankind does have a fear of the unknown. When it comes to dying, death, and the paranormal, that also holds true. It's both an abiding fascination and a macabre feeling of dread that influences humans when it comes to those things known as ghosts and the paranormal.

It is, then, always logical to look beneath the surface when it comes to hearing about a haunted house once belonging to a Witch, and that Witch's ghost is still lurking about, haunting the scene. Consider the situation for what it might be, or once was.

The Weeping Woman
Hollister, Missouri

Hollister is part of the Ozarks Mountains region in southwest Missouri and was settled in 1935. The town was named by Reuben Kirkham. After the 1970s, this colorful little town with buildings designed in the Tudor style closed down for the most part. The town did not revive until the 1990s with the growth of Branson, Missouri and Highway 65. The historic buildings are intact.

There are two ghosts of Confederate soldiers walking down the sidewalk of the buildings, seen during warm spring nights near sunset. A ghost of a weeping young woman is sometimes seen in the historic buildings area, walking very slowly with head bowed. On approach, she vanishes.

Spook Light Mystery
Hornet, Missouri

The Spook Light Mystery endures in Missouri and for many years was identified as the Joplin Ghost Light, or the Hornet Spook Light, among other names. If you can find road E50, you can find the Spook Light Road and see for yourself!

Hornet is a small community south of Joplin, Missouri, and is a prime location near the areas where the spook lights roam. Some people credit the origin of the spook lights as appearing during the time of the American Civil War. That the spook light continues to appear, and continues to endure and be witnessed by many people, is one of its greatest attractions for those interested in the paranormal. Its paranormal aspects are part of its intricate charm!

An interesting note on this Spook Light Mystery is the in depth investigation carried out by the Army Corps of Engineers. The examination of the areas where the spook lights were said to be seen were checked out, but no answer was found. The Army Corps of Engineers could not solve the Spook Light Mystery, as it's now referred to, and classified it as a mysterious light of unknown origin. To this day, that classification and definition serve best as no other logical answer has been discovered.

Too many people have witnessed this spook light, so it cannot be dismissed as marsh gas, reflection from car lights, pranks, ground lightning, small wood camp fires, firecrackers, or half a dozen other explanations that make no sense. I saw the spook light in the summer of 1959. I have no explanation for what it is either!

But it's there, and it does exist. And so far, it has not hurt anybody when it appears.

John Nelson Hanging
Palmyra, Missouri

John Nelson killed a couple in a most brutal fashion in 1869. Nelson's wife, Lavina, aided him in the killings. Sightings of John and Lavina Nelson near the murder scene have been seen, and they appear to be talking together. When Lavina laughs, the couple vanishes.

Headless Union Soldier
Lebanon, Missouri

Walking about in Lebanon, Missouri is an exercise in visiting a friendly town. It abounds in ghost stories, one of which involves a robbed and murdered peddler. The murder victim was Samuel Moritz and his murder took place close to the start of the American Civil War. His body remains were later found under a bridge. His ghost is said to haunt that bridge area to this day.

Some of the older homes hold stories of residual hauntings. An elderly man dressed in 1930s clothes wearing a wide-brimmed hat appears from nowhere on a front porch, and then walks towards the steps and vanishes. A teenager, perhaps a young woman in her senior year at high school, wearing late 1940s clothes is seen walking down a sidewalk near a house only to vanish as she passes that house. She has shoulder-length blonde hair and is smiling.

A man in his twenties with long, dark black hair and dressed in late 1960s style clothes is standing near a house on a corner. He is staring thoughtfully across the street at a house, but vanishes on approach.

The cemetery is reputed to be haunted by that of a headless Union soldier walking past grave markers, never stopping, but stepping along in a calculated fashion as if measuring distance. On approach the Union soldier ghost is said to vanish, leaving behind a scent of lavender face lotion.

Occupied by the Union forces, Lebanon was a war and railroad town, and prospered during those rough times. Some of the old hotel locations are also said to be haunted.

Captain William Anderson
Richmond, Missouri

One of the most ruthless Confederate guerrilla fighters during the American Civil War was a man named Captain William Anderson, whose nickname was "Bloody Bill." His killing sprees were known everywhere, and he killed without remorse.

Born in Missouri in 1840, he spent part of his early years in the state of Kansas. When war came, he was a solid part of Quantrill's Guerrillas, who were also known as Quantrill's Raiders.

Quantrill was another ruthless fighter and served the cause of the Confederacy with loyalty; yet, his killings and raids went beyond anything remotely considered normal under wartime conditions, and he relished in the pleasure of bloodletting. William Anderson would soon surpass him in bloodletting and killing.

Captain Anderson led the raid on Lawrence, Kansas in 1863, resulting in much mayhem and murder. He massacred a large group of Union soldiers in Centralia, Missouri on September 27, 1864. He personally killed the surviving Union soldiers with great relish and enjoyment. His psychotic actions instilled fear in friend and foe alike, although it's a well-known fact that his men were fiercely loyal to him and followed his orders without question.

In 1864, Anderson quarreled bitterly with Quantrill and left Quantrill's guerrilla fighters to form his own band of fighters. One of his recruits was a sixteen-year-old boy named Jesse James who would one day become an outlaw legend.

Anderson's bloody killings were not stopped until he was ambushed at Orrick, Missouri on October 27, 1864 and killed by bullets from the Union soldiers who surrounded him. His body was taken to Richmond, Missouri.

In Richmond, his dead body was abused and he was decapitated. His bloody head was hung on a pole for display. Later, his body was buried at an unmarked location outside Richmond. Whether his head was buried later, burned and thrown into a river, destroyed, or kept as a souvenir, remains a mystery.

His headless ghost is said to visit Orrick and Richmond in search of his decapitated head. Some researchers and writers claim William Anderson was not the man who died at Orrick, but an imposter who took his place when the battle was going against Anderson's band of guerrilla fighters. Knowing capture and death was imminent, Anderson escaped to safety, went out-of-state, and lived out his life elsewhere under an assumed name. His demise remains a curious piece of American Civil War history, and his ghost is still looking for its head.

Or perhaps, somebody else's ghost is looking for its head who was not the real Bloody Bill of Confederate legend, but a loyal look-alike who stepped into history at the wrong time and wrong place and died for that misstep! The American Civil War conflict in Missouri contains many strange, oftentimes macabre tales and hauntings.

The Ghost of Al Capone
Rockaway Beach, Missouri

Rockaway Beach, Missouri is located in the Ozark Mountains and is in an area of caves, trees, and scenic beauty. Founded during 1917, it is considered one of the earliest examples of a beautiful resort town in the United States. It's located ten miles northeast of Branson, Missouri.

There is an 1880s dressed male farmer seen walking near the beach; he mysteriously appears in October, carrying a wide-brimmed hat in his left hand, and then is not seen again the rest of the year. Shadow figures have been seen near the water's edge.

American gangster, Al Capone, is said to have vacationed here with his cronies. Since it is possible to see his hideaway across from the lake, it's been said that the ghost of Al Capone is seen walking the area during the summer.

The White Ghost Horse
Sparta, Missouri

A white horse has been seen in the older section of the town during the late winter months. It's without a saddle or bridle, and seems to be looking for some person or perhaps another horse companion. On approach, it fades from view and quickly vanishes.

Ghost Diver at Roubidoux Cave
Waynesville, Missouri

Waynesville, Missouri is located along the banks of Roubidoux Creek and its historic downtown is near the water. Roubidoux Spring Cave served as an encampment and rest point on the original Trail of Tears for the Cherokee Indians and other Native American groups.

Situated at the base of a steep cliff, the cave opening beckons to underwater divers. A ghost diver is oftentimes seen at the entrance.

This ghost is a young, petite woman with blonde hair. Her hairstyle is a 1960s pixie cut. Alone, she smiles, pulls the diving mask down over her face, raises her right arm, waves, and then plunges into the depths, never to return.

Haunted Bandstand
Stotts City, Missouri

Stotts City has an old bandstand that can be found at the corner of Mt. Vernon and Center Streets. Considered haunted, it's reputed to have a ghostly trumpet player. Sounds of a band have been heard at its location during warm summer nights. Shadow figures have been seen around it during the twilight hours.

Black Female Hangings

There were several hangings of black females in Missouri before the American Civil War, and usually these women were hanged for murder. Being slaves, they had no representation. Two examples said to relate to ghostly hauntings are Mary and Celia.

According to history, Mary was hanged for murder on September 30, 1838 in the jurisdiction of Ray County. Celia was hanged for murder in the jurisdiction of Greene County on December 21, 1855. The ghosts of the black women were once reputed to haunt the areas where they were hanged.

Ghost Waitress Marceline, Missouri

There is a ghost waitress in Marceline, Missouri who haunts the original Main Street Café.

This woman was a waitress who was murdered by her lover and has made her home in the Main Street Café. There are repeated residual hauntings in the area, and the appearances of what could be identified as intelligent hauntings depending on whom you receive the account from!

The story of her demise is that she was pregnant with child, was murdered by the railroad man who was the father of the child, and her body disposed of in an old well. The well, in which her body was dropped, sits under the restaurant.

The murder victim is also said to wear white and appears inside the restaurant as a waitress. Some stories refer to her as the waitress in white while other stories refer to her as the lady or woman in white. If you are interested in seeing this currently closed old restaurant site, the address is 116 South Kansas Avenue. Take a look inside the door and windows—you may just see the ghost of the murdered woman stacking dishes or carefully cleaning tabletops. If you do not see her, you may hear her.

For the tourist, Marceline, Missouri is a small town to fall in love with and had a great influence on cartoonist Walt Disney who lived in this town as a child. Disney based his intricate concept of Main Street, USA in Disneyland on the town of Marceline. Originally incorporated in 1888, this community became a railroad town because of its location for coal and fuel, and as a changeover point for railroad crews. The Atchison, Topeka, and Santa Fe Railroad opened tracks in Marceline in 1888.

Located in Linn County, it's well worth your time to visit and savor the main street setting of America's past. You might want to check out the City Hall at 116 Main Street for additional information. If you're near

Kansas City or St. Louis, and have the time, this is an ideal place to visit, photograph, and enjoy. Stay long enough to complete your visit with a nice ham sandwich lunch, potato salad, apple pie, and good strong coffee.

Outlaw Ghosts

Old vintage photograph of Jesse James.

It seems that almost everybody has a ghost tale about the outlaws roaming Missouri in spirit form, whether it's in the prisons they served time in, or various homes, caves, and hideaways they lived in, or as phantom riders. I am referring, of course, to those James and Younger gangs that lit up the public's imagination with their deeds.

There have been many movies about Jesse and Frank James. In 2007, a new and critically-acclaimed film came out in movie theaters starring Brad Pitt as Jesse James. Brad Pitt was raised in Springfield, Missouri and graduated from that city's school system. As long as the Jesse James legend lives, there will be movies about him.

Part Twenty: And Other Ghostly Tales

For the purposes of establishing a time frame on these outlaws and their legendary exploits, here is a date line on when they lived and died: Alexander Franklin James, 1843–1915; Jesse Woodson James, 1847–1882; Thomas Coleman Younger, 1844–1916; Robert Ewing Younger, 1853–1889; James Hardin Younger, 1848–1902; John Harrison Younger, 1851–1874.

Old vintage photograph of Bonnie & Clyde.

Another lively pair with adventures in 1930s Missouri should be mentioned, and that was the outlaw bank robbers, Bonnie Parker, 1910–1934, and Clyde Barrow, 1909–1934. The ghosts of Bonnie and Clyde have been seen in Platte City and Joplin. Controversy still rages over their deaths by ambush as they were never offered an opportunity to surrender by the law enforcement people who set out to kill them. Their ghosts have been seen at numerous sites in Missouri and elsewhere in the United States.

Ghosts of Wilson Creek National Battlefield, Republic, Missouri

Known in southern history as the Battle of Oak Hills, the American Civil War battle at Wilson's Creek, ten miles south of Springfield, was a hard-fought victory for the Confederacy. Located at 6424 West Farm Road 182 near Republic, Missouri, it was a bloody battle with high numbers of wounded on both sides. The Union soldiers killed were approximately 1,317 and the Southern soldiers killed were approximately 1,222. No historical documents are in existence that reveal how many more died from injuries and wounds received during the fighting. The battle took place on August 10, 1861, and is historically important as the first major battle of the American Civil War west of the Mississippi River.

The bloody battle also witnessed the death of Union general Nathaniel Lyon. Missouri ranks third as the most fought over state during the war. Although its sympathy was with the South and it had a keen wish to remain neutral, Missouri became a bloodbath for both sides.

Maintained today by the National Park Service, the area of battle is noted for its excellent shape and has become a favorite site for visitors. Ongoing archaeological digs and new finds continually turn up relics from the bloody encounter. Like much of the Springfield area in general, there are relics still to be found and much that is buried deep in the soil or covered by soil and structures. There are stories of buried weapons, rifles, ammunition, and money not yet found. One of the more famous stories is that a wagon carried rifles wrapped in heavy protective cloth and was buried to insure its secret location before the battle. To this day, it has never been found, and remains an elusive mystery to be solved.

Ghost stories abound concerning Wilson's Creek and its surrounding area. Numerous accounts of residual hauntings have been shared privately and publicly since the battle was fought. Many sightings of ghost soldiers involved in this famous battle have been seen.

There is indeed an eerie feeling about the place, which intensifies with the approach of evening. Evening time at Wilson's Creek battlefield is the time of the shadow figures.

The American Civil War has inspired much paranormal literature, including fiction, nonfiction, and movies. Those interested in pursuing this search will find much to intrigue and entertain them!

American Civil War Ghost Sites

There are numerous Civil War battle sites in Missouri, and many of them are reputed to have ghostly apparitions, hauntings, and other paranormal activity. A death by violence leaves its mark on a battlefield. This explains the immense, enduring number of hauntings on battlefields and related areas throughout the world.

Overall, Missouri is considered one of the bloodiest war battlefields between the North and the South. Some battles and skirmishes in Missouri spilled over into neighboring states and territories. Here is a partial listing of recorded battles and skirmishes in Missouri: Kansas City, Westport, Lexington, Centralia, St. Louis, Jefferson City, Marshall, Boonville, Sedalia, Osceola, Nevada, Rolla, Humansville, Palmyra, Pilot Knob, Lamar, Stockton, Greenfield, Marshfield, Hartville, Cape Girardeau, Carthage, Sherwood, Springfield, Wilson's Creek, Fort Lawrence, Ozark, Neosho, Newtonia, Forsyth, and West Plains. This list does not include those many areas that were involved in minor skirmishes, or where deaths were not recorded or either forgotten or unknown.

Although the North considered Missouri a hard-fought prize and a border state occupied by the Union, it was also claimed by the South as a legitimate Confederate state with an established Confederate state government. One example of how Confederates were treated in Missouri by Union forces is found in the massacre that took place in the town of Palmyra, located in Marion County, Missouri. Ten Missouri southerners were to be executed without due process of law by Union General John McNeil. He selected the most educated, respected, and influential citizens of Palmyra to be executed because a Union informer named Andrew Allsman turned up missing. On October 18, 1862, these ten unarmed, innocent men were massacred by Union troops, and as a result of this atrocity, President Abraham Lincoln personally promoted McNeil to Brigadier General of United States Volunteers for McNeil's loyalty and bravery. Today, a memorial is found in the city in honor of the ten murdered men. It's reputed that the ghosts of these murdered Missouri southerners still haunt Palmyra and Marion County, a lovely area once home to the Fox and Sac Indian tribes until the 1700s when it was settled by the French. For an interesting visit, check out Palmyra, Missouri, and feel its history.

Despite the conflicts, whether moral, spiritual, ethical, personal, political, or economic, Missouri was full of brave, small town Southern men and women who fought for the Confederacy. There are many stories about the atrocities of the American Civil War from both the Union and the Confederacy. Palmyra, Missouri was but one setting for such horrors. There are too many to list.

Reading about what is oftentimes defined as the war for Southern Independence, I came to understand more fully the paranormal aspects and why people in the United States are still seeing residual and intelligent hauntings of ghosts from the American Civil War. This section of American history was a traumatic time in which people were fighting and dying for a way of life they cherished, and the conflict centered on which dream was to be fulfilled and allowed to prosper, and which dream was to be destroyed, forced into exile.

Researching the massive material available on Missouri during the American Civil War and the war in general, I came across numerous interesting books including the intriguing nonfiction book, *The South Was Right* by James Ronald Kennedy and Walter Donald Kennedy, and the many excellent books written by the American historian, William C. Davis. I was amazed by the documented information concerning how many former black slaves and freed slaves of their own free will fought in the Confederacy for the cause of Southern Independence. There are many other historians whose writings I found fascinating. Since this was my initial exposure to the American Civil War and its cause, I would suggest, whatever one's personal preference is, that he or she not overlook reading these unusual books with their interesting bibliographies and extensive notes. I found reading about the actual background and social themes of the American Civil War an education in and of itself.

For those interested in the logical cause for the American Civil War, I would suggest reading the following book, which opened my eyes to what did happen: *When in the Course of Human Events* by historian, Charles Adams. This non-fiction book was published in 2000, and the author states with docmentation and research that slavery was not the issue of the American Civil War. The issue was unfair taxation, and that is the true reason the South seceded and the war started. The American Civil War was not fought over slavery, but was fought over three things: territory, resources, and revenue. Other historians of note to consider for reading would include Gary W. Gallagher and George C. Rable. These writers may not be politically correct, but they are honest in giving the truth to readers about the American Civil War. I am glad I discovered their books.

I came to the conclusion after my research that the Civil War was a struggle between two distinctly separate lifestyles, the Northern perspective and the Southern perspective. Each had its own way of life, and each followed its own destiny to victory or defeat. It's always important to remember that ghosts are ghosts, regardless of their color, sex, beliefs, or ethnic origins. It's also always important to remember that history is written initially by the victors, not the losers. Nobody should ever be owned by another and nobody should ever become a slave to another. Slavery of any kind is the cruelest form of spiritual degradation and should not be allowed to exist anywhere for any reason. Corrections to slavery must be made, and atoned for, even in the case of ghosts whenever possible. To set free a haunted soul or correct an injustice to a person's existence when he or she was once alive should be and must be done.

A good example of this is the horrid things written about American writer Edgar Allan Poe (1809–1849), which were not corrected completely until over a hundred years after his death. As my late grandmother, Archie T. Firestone told me many times, "In the end, the truth comes out, however painful that truth is. Integrity will and does whip the ass of any lie, and the person who tells the lie!" Grandmother Firestone was a small town Southern woman born in Missouri, who lived in Missouri all of her life and always gave a person a third chance to be good. She believed the American Civil War should never have happened and called it a war of greed and she believed the war was not fought over slavery. She also believed that all children deserved the loving guidance of a loving mother and father, that you can't teach ideas to a child if that child is hungry and has an empty stomach, that the human soul is immortal, that religion is a personal matter, and that ghosts exist, among other ideas. Thanks, Grandma Firestone, and rest in peace!

Let me share this personal note about my grandmother. She did not often speak of ghosts or seeing ghosts, but she had a very old cure for bad spirits that came to visit a home from time to time. Ghost hunters may wish to note this down in their logbooks for future reference. Grandmother Firestone would take a small saucer, made of clear glass or white glass, and then fill it to the brim with white vinegar. She would place that full saucer of white vinegar in a high place, such as on top of a refrigerator or in whatever room of the house seemed troubled. As the white vinegar evaporated, so did the power and presence of the ghostly spirit until that ghostly spirit was gone. It worked for her. There are many approaches to eliminating hauntings or ghostly presences. That is one way, call it the Archie T. Firestone way, passed down to her as a child from members of her family.

A ghost hunter by whatever name and design cannot be expected to come riding up dressed in the proverbial white clothes, white hat, and white cloak, riding on a white horse to save the day for a ghost! But that ghost hunter can do whatever possible when and where feasible to understand those ghosts and put them gently to rest and join the White Light if she or he can. That would be a genuine gift of kindness from the living to the haunted dead. To help a ghost pass over and go on, that is a true gift of kindness because being a ghost is being a slave to a given moment in existential time without having any answers to personal questions as to why he or she is a ghost. There is also the consideration of some who would say, let the dead bury the dead. In that case, who then buries the dead pallbearers?

Life and death as symbols with separate realities are indeed existential doorways to different dimensions. We each go through each door, one way or another.

French Ghosts

When Napoleon of France made the Louisiana Purchase happen with agreeable American input, it was to change the face and character of early settlements in the United States. It did not stop the influx of French explorers, gamblers, settlers, and missionaries; it merely made it possible for them to enter without interference. This could also apply to other large ethnic and foreign groups that settled the USA.

That there is an abundance of French ghosts spread out across what is today the United States of America is not surprising. Research will reveal that there are many French men, women, and children appearing as ghosts in numerous hauntings, ghost sightings, and paranormal occurrences.

In looking at our ancestors, distant past, and recent past, it is interesting to see where there heritage roots derive from.

Missouri does have its share of French ghosts. Other groups are equally represented. If you encounter a ghostly situation in Missouri where you cannot understand what the ghost or presence is saying, maybe that is because it is being spoken or uttered in the French language. Something to think about!

Ghost Towns and Underwater Cemeteries

There are settlements, villages, towns, mining sites, soldier camp sites, caves, abandoned haunted houses, and cemeteries that no longer exist in Missouri for one reason or another, and their remembered existence and location is usually passed down by word of mouth. In attempting to compile such a list, it's necessary to talk to many people, and usually, each person has a different interpretation. This is a fine example of the Sociological Theory of Paradoxical Perception: Three people standing at three separate locations each witness an automobile accident, and when asked what they each saw, each one gives a different perspective on the details witnessed. Likewise, a site may have once been in a given area, but as to what is there now or a precise way for reaching it, that may be another story all together in trying to locate it.

If you are interested in Missouri ghost towns, find old state or road maps and compare them to a new map. Here are some ghost town locations for you to consider for further research: Goldman, Missouri; Arlington, Missouri; Hamburg, Missouri; Monark Springs, Missouri; Possum Trot, Missouri; and Xenia, Missouri. As to possible remains of towns and cemeteries that may or may not be underwater, you may wish to research the following areas: Truman Reservoir, Table Rock Lake, Pomme de Terre Lake, Smithville Lake, Mark Twain Reservoir, Lake Wappapello, and Lake of the Ozarks. There may be other areas.

Not all cemeteries are moved to a new location when faced with being permanently placed underwater. Why? Because not all sites may be remembered accurately as to precise location, or nobody remembers them. As a result, these burial sites are accidentally overlooked; this is nobody's fault.

Time does ironic things to human memories, as well as to where something is thought to be placed at any given setting in a landscape. Landscapes do not necessarily change, but where something is placed or buried on that designated landscape can, and do. When people abandon an area, they take their memories with them, and with the passage of time, those who come after them oftentimes sadly forget those people and their memories. There is no place truer for that than in the throwaway society of the United States, where one memory is quickly supplanted by new ones in the course of a day. So much is lost simply because there is so much to remember in our technological society!

The United States is constantly reinventing itself as a nation, and that includes its history and memories of what went before. What is lost is lost, and that applies to historical sites. That loss is sad, and it is great, because there comes a reflective moment when all that is left is a keen feeling of nostalgia for those lost times, and words on paper to remind us of what we have lost. Americans too often destroy themselves by destroying their relics. America as a nation has forgotten now to preserve. For a society to destroy its relics through mishap or missed opportunity is to destroy its ability to leave a solid heritage for its descendants, and in many cases, that is what is happening in the USA today.

Just maybe, that is one of the numerous possible reasons why the living have ghosts, paranormal occurrences, and hauntings to remind them of some specific incident in the past. There are many ghosts around to remind the living, if only we would take the time to observe and learn the reasons why there are hauntings, and paranormal activity. We are never alone. There will always be ghosts accompanying us on our journeys.

Ghost Hunting Tips

Getting There, Being There, and Encountering Personal Discoveries

I have been asked over the years about getting there, being there, and personal discovery. I enjoy physical, on-site examinations of an area whenever feasible.

There are also other avenues to pursue if you wish to undertake the training required to do them. You can astral travel and you can do remote viewing. Each one is a variation of techniques that will make the various aspects of time travel available to you on a personal level. Each requires effort and determination to achieve.

Look through the recommended reading section at the end of this book and see if there is something that intrigues you! Please feel free to browse through and read my published book reviews, essays, articles, and "Bide One's Time" column found on Ghostvillage.com for additional ideas.

Lee Prosser meditating with his cat.

Also, there are numerous books in publication or at used bookstores dealing with the subject of astral travel, and how to approach and train yourself for astral travel. As to becoming proficient in the skill of remote viewing, there is an abundance of material available. If you want to pursue remote viewing, you might want to consider an important work titled, *The Remote Viewing Training Course: Principles and Technologies of Coordinate Remote Viewing* by David Morehouse; this is published by Sounds True and contains guided instruction towards becoming a proficient remote viewer.

As to pursing time travel, the techniques of astral travel or remote viewing will get you there. You won't be able to change history, but consider this paranormal aspect: You may be able to see the actual occurrence that made it possible for the appearance of a ghost or specific haunting to take place! Much like arriving at the given moment the historical fact unfolds. It's up to the individual, and what it is the individual is seeking to find when getting there, being there, and when encountering personal discoveries.

Internet Resources for Ghost Hunters

Here are some Internet sites for ghost hunters in search of additional information and places of interest. With careful research, the reader will discover many more, including various organizations and universities that have some connection directly related to the supernatural, the paranormal, and ghosts.

Also remember to visit public libraries, state historical societies, local historical societies, newspapers, senior citizen organizations, folklore societies, and museums in your ongoing search for available information. You will be surprised with what you turn up in the course of a friendly conversation, or in reading! It may well lead you to an overlooked ghost location, haunting, or paranormal activity waiting to be discovered by you! Good luck in compiling your own list of ghost hunting resources!

www.ghostvillage.com

www.ghosthunter.com

www.ghostresearch.org

www.ghoststore.net.

www.hauntings.com

www.mindreader.com

www.ghosttowns.com

www.theshadowlands.net/ghost

www.nationalghosthunters.com/investigations.html

www.ghots.net

www.prarieghosts.com

www.the-atlantic-paranormal-society.com

www.hollowhill.com

www.ghostweb.com

www.jeffdwyer.com

www.ispr.net/home.html

www.ghosthunting.com

www.ghostweb.com

Musings from the Midnight Hour

We have come to the end of this journey, and I sincerely appreciate your having traveled along with me. I hope you have enjoyed this book. Perhaps there will be another one in the future.

In the meantime, please remember to be on the lookout in your own personal life for anything happening in the manner of hauntings, paranormal occurrences, and ghosts! Thank you for going on walkabout with me through Missouri, one of the most haunted states in the United States.

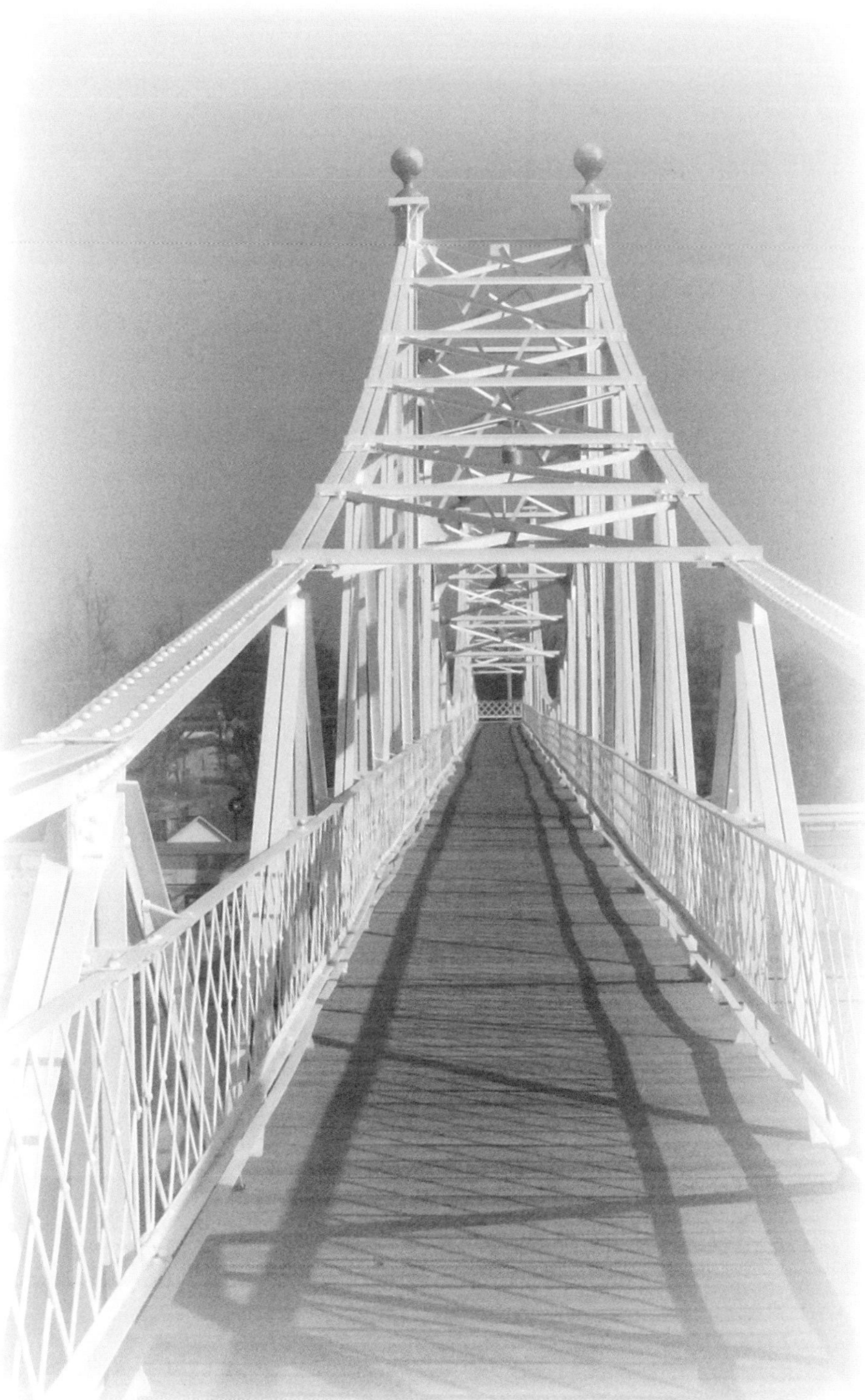

Suggested Readings

Andrews, Ted. *How to Uncover Your Past Lives*. Woodbury, Minnesota: Llewellyn Publications, 2002.

Baldwin, Barbara J., Garretson, Jerri, Madl, Linda, and McGathy, Sherri L. *Trespassing Time: Ghost Stories from the Prairie*. Manhattan, Kansas: Ravenstone Press, 2005.

Belanger, Jeff. *The Ghost Files*. Franklin Lakes, New Jersey: New Page Books, 2007.
Ghosts of War: Restless Spirits of Soldiers, Spies, and Saboteurs. Franklin Lakes, New Jersey: New Page Books, 2006.
The World's Most Haunted Places. Franklin Lakes, New Jersey: New Page Books, 2004.
Communicating With the Dead: Reach Beyond the Grave. Franklin Lakes, New Jersey: New Page Books, 2005.
Our Haunted Lives: True Life Ghost Encounters. Franklin Lakes, New Jersey: New Page Books, 2006

Berry, Earl. *Pioneer Life and Pioneer Families of the Ozarks*. Cassville, Missouri: Litho Printers, 1980.

Bruce, Robert & Mercer, Brian. *Mastering Astral Projection: 90-Day Guide to Out-of-Body Experience*. Woodbury, Minnesota: Llewellyn Publications, 2004.

Buckland, Raymond. *Buckland's Book of Spirit Communications, Second Edition*. Woodbury, Minnesota: Llewellyn Publications, 2004.

Castaneda, Carlos. *The Wheel of Time*. New York, New York: Washington Square Press, 1998.

Churchill, Winston S. *The American Civil War*. London, England: Cassell & Company, 1961.

Suggested Readings

Churton, Tobias. *The Gnostics*. New York, New York: Barnes & Noble. 1997.
Gnostic Philosophy. Rochester, Vermont: Inner Traditions, 2005.

Cohen, Daniel. *Civil War Ghosts*. New York, New York: Scholastic, 1999.

Conway, D. J. *The Mysterious, Magical Cat*. Woodbury, Minnesota: Llewellyn Publications, 1998.

Curran, Bob. *Encyclopedia of the Undead: A Field Guide to the Creatures That Cannot Rest in Peace*. Franklin Lakes, New Jersey: New Page Books, 2006.

Danelek, J. Allan. *The Case For Ghosts: An Objective Look at the Paranormal*. Woodbury, Minnesota: Llewellyn Publications, 2006.

Davidson, Wilma. *Spirit Rescue: A Simple Guide to Talking with Ghosts and Freeing Earthbound Spirits*. Woodbury, Minnesota: Llewellyn Publications, 2006.

Donovan, Timothy H. *The American Civil War*. Wayne, New Jersey and New York, New York: Avery Publishing Group, 2000.

DuQuette, Lon Milo. *The Magic of Aleister Crowley*. York Beach, Maine: Weiser Books, 2003.

Dunwich, Gerina. *A Witch's Guide to Ghosts and the Supernatural*. Franklin Lakes, New Jersey: New Page Books, 2002.
Dunwich's Guide to Gemstone Sorcery: Using Stones for Spells, Amulets, Rituals, and Divination. Franklin Lakes, New Jersey: New Page Books, 2003.
Phantom Felines and Other Ghostly Animals. New York, New York: Citadel Press, 2006.
Your Magical Cat: Feline Magic, Lore, and Worship. New York, New York: Citadel Press, 2000.

The Concise Lexicon of the Occult. New York, New York: Citadel Press, 1990.

Ebon, Martin. *They Knew The Unknown*. New York, New York: The World Publishing Company, 1971.

Eynden, Rose Vanden. *So You Want to Be a Medium: A Down-to-Earth Guide*. Woodbury, Minnesota: Llewellyn Publications, 2006.

Feather, Fran Dancing, and Rita Robinson. *Exploring Native American Wisdom*. Franklin Lakes, New Jersey: New Page Books, 2003.

Filan, Kenaz. *The Haitian Vodou Handbook: Protocols for Riding with the Law*. Rochester, Vermont: Destiny Books, 2007.

Fiore, Edith. *The Unquiet Dead*. New York, New York: Dolphin, 1987.

Floyd, E. Randall. *In the Realm of Ghosts and Hauntings*. Augusta, Georgia: Harbor House, 2002.

Fodor, Nandor. *Between Two Worlds*. West Nyack, New York: Parker Publishing Company, 1964.

Gray-Cobb, Maiya & Geof. *Angels: The Guardians of Your Destiny*. Huntsville, Arkansas: Ozark Mountain Publishing, 2008.

Guiley, Rosemary Ellen. *The Encyclopedia of Ghosts and Spirits, Second Edition*. New York, New York: Checkmark Books, 2000.

Hardinge, Emma. *History of Modern Spiritualism*. New York, New York: University Books, 1970. (Reprint of the 1870 edition.)

Harryman, Wilma Groves. *Ozark Mountain Girl*. Leawood, Kansas: Leathers Publishing, 1997.

Suggested Readings

Harvey, John. *Photography and Spirit.* London, England: Reaktion Books Ltd., 2007.

Hawes, Jason and Wilson, Grant, with Michael Jan Friedman. *Ghost Hunting: True Stories of Unexplained Phenomena from The Atlantic Paranormal Society.* New York, New York: Simon & Schuster, 2007.

Holzer, Hans. Ghosts: *True Encounters with the World Beyond.* New York, New York: Black Dog & Leventhal Publishers, 1997.
Real Hauntings: America's True Ghost Stories. New York, New York: Barnes & Noble, Inc., 1995.
True Ghost Stories. New York, New York: Dorset Press, 2001.
Window to the Past: How Psychic Time Travel Reveals the Secrets of History. New York, New York: Citadel Press, 1993.

Honigman, Andrew (editor). *My Proof of Survival: Personal Accounts of Contact with the Hereafter.* Woodbury, Minnesota: Llewellyn Publications, 2003.

Hill, Gary Leon. *People Who Don't Know They're Dead.* York Beach, Maine: Weiser Books, 2005.

Kachuba, John. *Ghosthunters: On the Trail of Mediums, Dowsers, Spirit Seekers, and Other Investigators of America's Paranormal World.* Franklin Lakes, New Jersey: New Page Books, 2007.

Kenyon, J. Douglas. *Forbidden History.* Rochester, Vermont: Bear & Company, 2005.
Forbidden Religion. Rochester, Vermont: Bear & Company, 2006.

Koltuv, Barbara Black. *The Book of Lilith.* Berwick, Maine: Nicolas-Hays, 1986.

Kubler-Ross, Elizabeth. *The Wheel of Life.* New York, New York: Scribner, 1997.

LeShan, Lawrence. *The Medium, the Mystic, and the Physicist*. New York, New York: Viking Press, 1974.

Leek, Sybil. *Reincarnation: The Second Chance*. New York, New York: Stein and Day, 1974.

Lowry, Thomas P. *The Stories the Soldiers Wouldn't Tell: Sex in the Civil War*. Mechanisburg, Pennsylvania: Stackpole Books, 1994.

Macy, Mark. *Spirit Faces: Truth About the Afterlife*. York Beach, Maine: Weiser Books, 2006.

Malachi, Tau. *Gnosis of the Cosmic Christ*. Woodbury, Minnesota: Llewellyn, 2005.

Marsh, Clint. *The Mentalist's Handbook: An Explorer's Guide to Astral, Spirit, and Psychic Worlds*. Newburyport, Massachusetts: Red Wheel/Weiser, 2008.

Martello, Leo Louis. *Witchcraft: The Old Religion*. New York, New York: Citadel Press, 1991.

Martinez, Susan B. *The Psychic Life of Abraham Lincoln*. Franklin Lakes, New Jersey: New Page Books, 2007.

Kathleen McConnell. *Don't Call Them Ghosts: The Spirit Children of Fontaine Manse*. Woodbury, Minnesota: Llewellyn Publications, 2004.

McTeer, J. E. *Fifty Years as a Low Country Witch Doctor*. Columbia, South Carolina: The R.L. Bryan Company, 1976.

Morehouse, David. *The Remote Viewing Training Course: Principles and Techniques of Coordinate Remote Viewing*. Boulder, Colorado: Sounds True, 2004.

Suggested Readings

Moura, Ann. *Origins of Modern Witchcraft: The Evolution of a World Religion*. Woodbury, Minnesota: Llewellyn, 2000.

Morley, Christopher. *The Haunted Bookshop*. New York, New York: Barnes & Noble Books, 2004.

Nicholson, Shirley. *Shamanism*. Wheaton, Illinois: The Theosophical Publishing House, 1987.

Offutt, Jason. *Haunted Missouri: A Ghostly Guide to the Show-Me State's Most Spirited Spots*. Kirksville, Missouri: Truman State University Press, 2007.

Owens, Elizabeth. *Spiritualism & Clairvoyance for Beginners: Simple Techniques to Develop Your Psychic Abilities*. Woodbury, Minnesota: Llewellyn Publications, 2005.
How to Communicate with Spirits. Woodbury Minnesota: Llewellyn Publications, 2001.

Price, Edwin. *Haints, Witches, and Boogers: Tales from Upper East Tennessee*. Winston, Salem, North Carolina: John F. Blair, Publisher, 1992.

Prosser, Lee. *Isherwood, Bowles, Vedanta, Wicca, and Me*. Lincoln, Nebraska: Writer's Club, 2001.
Night Tigers. Lincoln, Nebraska: Writer's Club, 2002.

Rain, Mary Summer. *Eclipse*. Charlottesville, Virginia: Hampton Books, 1999.
Soul Sounds. Charlottesville, Virginia: Hampton Books, 1992.

Ramsland, Katherine. *Ghost: A Firsthand Account into the World of the Paranormal Activity*. New York, New York: St. Martin's Press, 2001.

RavenWolf, Silver. *Mind of Light: Secrets of Energy, Magick & Manifestation*. Woodbury, Minnesota: Llewellyn Publications, 2006.

Ring, Kenneth and Valarino, Evelyn Elsaesser. *Lessons from the Light: What we can Learn from the Near-Death Experience*. Needham, Massachusetts: Moment Point Press, 2000.

Rosa, Joseph G. *Age of the Gunfighter: Men and Weapons on the Frontier, 1840–1900*. Norman, Oklahoma: University of Oklahoma Press, 1995.

Schmitt, Jean Claude. *Ghosts in the Middle Ages: The Living and the Dead in Medieval Society*. Chicago, Illinois: University of Chicago Press, 1998.

Schnabel, Jim. *Remote Viewers: The Secret History of America's Psychic Spies*. New York, New York: Dell, 1997.

Slate, Joe H. *Beyond Reincarnation: Experience Your Past Lives & Lives Between Lives*. Woodbury, Minnesota: Llewellyn Publications, 2005.

Stavish, Mark. *Between the Gates: Lucid Dreaming, Astral Projection, and the Body of Light in Western Esotericism*. San Francisco, California: Weiser, 2008.

Steiger, Brad. *Real Ghosts, Restless Spirits, and Haunted Places*. Canton, Michigan: Visible Ink Press, 2003.

Stemman, Roy. *Spirits and Spirit Worlds*. New York, New York: Doubleday, 1963.

Tyson, Donald. *How to Make and Use a Magic Mirror: Psychic Windows Into New Worlds*. Custer, Washington: Phoenix Publishing, Inc., 1995.

Vaughan, Thomas. *Works of Thomas Vaughan, Mystic and Alchemist.* Edited by Arthur E. Waite. New Hyde Park, New York: University Books, 1969.

Wagner, Margaret E. *The American Civil War.* New York, New York: Harry N. Abrams, Inc., 2006.

Walter, Philippe. *Christianity: The Origins of a Pagan Religion.* Rochester, Vermont: Inner Traditions, 2003.

Watts, Alan. *In My Own Way: An Autobiography, 1915–1965.* Novato, California: New World, 2001.

Weisberg, Barbara. *Talking to the Dead: Kate and Maggie Fox and the Rise of Spiritualism.* New York, New York: Harper. 2004.

Wicker, Christine. *Lily Dale: The True Story of the Town That Talks to the Dead.* San Francisco, California: Harper, 2003.

INDEX

Abou Ben Adhem Shrine Mosque, 43
Adams – Gehm House, 99
Aid-Hodgson Mill, 141
American Civil War, 11, 22, 24, 31, 32, 47, 48, 55, 63, 64, 71, 75, 76, 78, 85, 93, 94, 95, 101, 103, 121, 122, 127, 130, 131, 132, 139, 140, 143, 144, 145, 146, 150, 153, 154, 155, 156, 160, 161, 162, 164, 166, 167, 168, 169, 177, 178, 184
American Indian, 11, 20, 42, 48, 53, 55, 68, 70, 76, 94, 96, 97, 102, 104, 112, 125, 136, 142, 144, 146, 154, 156, 163, 168
American Wild West, 24, 76, 78, 123, 124
Arlington, Missouri, 171
Ash Grove, Missouri, 83
astral travel, 119, 173, 177, 181, 183
Atchison, Topeka and Santa Fe Railway, 164
Aurora, Missouri, 71, 72, 73
Ax decapitation, 111

Bachardy, Don, 3, 24
Bald Knobbers, 75, 81, 82, 103
Baldwin Park, 71
bandstand, 17, 139, 141, 163
Baptist Church, 54, 140
banshee, 50, 112, 157
Barker – Karpis Gang, 84
Barker, Kate "Ma," 83, 84

Barrow, Clyde, 166
Bates, Moses, 111
Battle of Carthage, 143
Battle of Oak Hills, 166
Berry Cemetery, 83
Bennett Springs State Park, 154
Big Piney River, 157
Billy the Kid, 9, 123, 124
Black Female Hangings, 164
Black River, 142
Blanchette, Louis, 115
Bluegrass Farm, 53
Bluff Dweller's Cave, 9, 135, 136
Boegel and Hine Mill, 84
Bolin, Alf, 75, 155, 156
Bolivar, Missouri, 150
Bonnie & Clyde, 122, 166
Boonville, Missouri, 145
Booth, Christopher Saint, 45
Booth, Phillip Adrian, 45
Bowring, Senator Eva, 144
Branson, Missouri, 75, 76, 77, 78, 79, 156, 159, 162
Branson, Rueben, 75
Brooke Hillary, 56
Browning Museum, 135, 136
Buckland, Raymond, 158, 177
Burge, Elle A., 42
Burge School of Nursing, 42
Butterfield Overland Stage, 31
Buttons, Red, 140

Cameron Cave, 111
Campbell, John Polk, 31
Capone, Al, 162, 163
Carradine, John 135

Index

Carrington Hall, 61
Carthage, Missouri, 143
Cassville, Missouri, 156, 177
Central Assembly Christian Life Center, 125
Central High School, 41, 42
Central Methodist University, 146
Centralia, Missouri, 162, 167
Chadwick, Missouri, 81, 82, 155
Chaney, Jr., Lon, 135
Chappel, Major R. B., 49
Cherokee Cave, 96
Cherry Blossom Festival, 100
Chest Hospital, 152
Chetanananda, Swami, 3
"Children of the Grave," 45, 46
Christian Church Hospital, 128, 129
Christian, Peter A., 49
Civil War Cemetery, 36, 41, 44, 61, 62, 63, 64, 93, 94, 95, 101, 131, 132, 139, 141, 145, 146, 161
Clairaudience, 106
Clairaugustine, 106
Clairsentience, 106
Clairvoyance, 106
Cole, Hannah, 145
Colonial Hotel, 20, 21
Commercial Street, 14, 29, 31
Confederate Capitol of Missouri, 156
Connor Hotel, 124
Contact with the past, 51
Conway, Missouri, 102
Cooper County, Missouri, 145
Corey, Wendell, 24
Cox Hospital North, 42

Crane, Missouri, 143
Crown Center, 130, 131
Cruikshank, John, J., 111
Cummings, Robert, 122

Danforth, Martin, 50
Davisville, Missouri, 150
Deadman's Pond, 9, 153
Dent County Courthouse, 139
Devil's Elbow, Missouri, 157
Diggins, Missouri, 48
Disney, Walt, 164
Disneyland, 164
Dixon, Missouri, 151
Doling, James Marshall, 54, 138
Doling Park, 17, 18, 20, 22
Doniphan, Missouri, 142
Dreamland Theater, 113
Dunwich, Gerina, 158
Drury University, 56, 58, 59

Earp, Wyatt, 157
Eastern Star, 54, 138
Elwood Cemetery, 130
English Cave, 96
English, Ezra O., 96
Evangel University, Evangel College, 56, 57, 58

Fair Grove, Missouri, 85, 86, 87, 88, 89
Farm Road 94, 53
Fayette Courthouse, 146
Fayette, Missouri 146
Fassnight Park, 25, 26, 27, 28, 34
Fonda, Henry, 135
Forsyth, Missouri, 103

Index

Fort Leonard Wood, 137
Fox Theater, Joplin, Missouri, 124
Fox Theater, Springfield, Missouri, 22, 24, 25
French Colonial Village, 117
French Ghosts in Missouri, 170, 171
Frisco Railroad, 151

Galena, Missouri, 48, 105, 106, 107, 108, 109, 144, 153
Garden House Bed & Breakfast, 111
Gehm, Henry, 99
German soldier prisoners of war, 45
Gertie, mechanical gypsy lady, 15
ghost chef, 67
ghost diver, 163
ghost male trumpet player, 68
ghost waitress, 164
Giboney brothers, John Thomas and James, 17
Gillioz, M. E., 103, 113
Gillioz Theater, 34, 35, 113, 114
Gilmore Octagonal Barn, 83
Goldenrod Showboat, 116
Goldman, Missouri, 171
Gotti, John, 70
Gratiot Street Prison, 93
Great Cyclone of 1896, 92
Greenlawn Memorial Gardens, 44, 45
green-eyed lady ghost, 105
grist mill, 85
Grove, The, 68

Hanging Barn, 145
Hamburg, Missouri, 171
Hannibal, Missouri, 111, 112
Hardin Park, 138
Harper, Tess, 60
haunted attic, 58, 60, 100, 125, 140, 142, 143, 152
haunted basement, 22, 25, 30, 31, 42, 43, 58, 60, 66, 77, 92, 122, 129, 143, 152
haunted bridges, 17, 26, 28, 30, 31, 83, 85, 86, 87, 90, 97, 98, 103, 104, 105, 114, 138, 141, 145, 161
haunted rings, 11
haunted houses, 11
haunted keys, 11
Headless Union Soldier, 161
Heer's Department Store, 32
Hickok, Will Bill, 36
Highway K, 154
Highway 13, 48, 50, 150
Highway 44, 123
Highway 65, 85, 159
Highway 125, 90
Highway 160, 83
Highway 248, 105
Holland Building, 32
Hollister, Missouri 159
Homer G. Phillips Hospital, 9
Hornet, Missouri, 160
Hospital 2, 99
hotel ghosts and hauntings, 20, 21
House of Lords, 122
Houston Lake, 134
Howard County, 146
Hubble, Edwin P., Hubble Telescope, 101
Hughes, Langston, 122

187

Hull, Henry, 135
Huston, John, 144

Indian Cave, 156
Indian Creek, 154
intelligent haunting, 11, 36, 37, 38, 39, 40, 42, 45, 46, 51, 52, 55, 87, 95, 100, 105, 113, 111, 116, 119, 120, 127, 147, 152, 164, 166, 167, 168
intuition, 106
intuitive, 106
Iron Mountain, 93
Isbell, Bud, 49
Isherwood, Christopher, 24
Italian ghost, 99
Iturbi, Jose, 56

J. C. Penney building, 25
James, Frank, 75, 117, 144, 165
James, Jesse, 75, 117, 123, 124, 135, 144, 162, 165
James River, 48, 105
Jasper County, 143
Jefferson Barracks National Cemetery, 93
Jefferson Street Footbridge, 30, 31
Jennings, Waylon, 77
Joplin, Missouri, 121, 122
Joplin, Reverend Harris, 121
Joplin, Scott, 145
Joplin Supply Company, 122, 125

Kansas City, Missouri, 48, 12, 128
Katy Depot, 145

Kelly, Nancy, 135
Kemm, Johnny 17
Kennedy, John F., 20
Kerouac, Jack, 106
Kingshighway Boulevard, 97
Kittrell, Solomon, 142
Knob Noster, Missouri, 145

Lady Bushwhackers, 144
LaCourse, Charlotte, 120
LaFayette, Marquis de, 145, 146
LaFayette Square, 100
LaFonte, Jean Baptiste, 120
Lake of the Ozarks, 171
Lamar, Missouri, 157
Landers Theater, 32, 33
laughing red-headed woman ghost, 71, 72
Lawrence County Mining sites, 71
lead mines hauntings, 143
Lebanon, Missouri, 161
Lee, Christopher, 46
Lemp, Adam, 96
Lemp, Charles, 92
Lemp, Julia, 92
Lemp Mansion, 92
Lemp Theater, 96
"Les Petites Cotes," 115
library ghost at Missouri State University, 60
library ghosts at Public Library, Springfield, Missouri, 66, 67
Liberty Memorial, 127
limestone quarries hauntings, 143
Little Dixie, 147
Little Dixie Region of Missouri, 146
Lone Rock Cemetery, 154

Lunatic Asylum State Hospital No. 3, 144
Lynch, William Henry, 75
Lyon, Nathaniel, 166

Magic City, 147
Main Street, USA, 164
Maple Park Cemetery, 36, 37, 38, 39, 40, 41
Marceline, Missouri, 164
Mark Twain Cave, 111
Mark Twain Lake, 137
Marshfield, Missouri, 101, 102, 167
Martello, Leo Louis, 158
Marvel Cave, 75
Masonic Memorial, 44
Masters, John, 31
Maxwell, Paulita, 123
Mayfield, Ella, 144
McAuley, Catherine, 68
McBride, Mary Margaret, 137
McCullagh Hall, 58
Memorial Gardens, 142, 144
Meramec Springs Park, 139
Messerli, Godfrey, 26
Mexico, Missouri, 138
Mississippi River, 92, 93, 111, 117, 166
Missouri Ozarks, 14
Missouri Pacific train wreck of 1904, 144
Missouri Rehab Center, 152
Missouri River, 115, 116, 127
Missouri State University, 60, 61, 56
Missouri Veterans Home and Cemetery, 139, 152
Mitchell, Cameron, 78. 79

Mitchum, Robert, 113
Moberly, Missouri, 147
Monark Springs, Missouri, 171
Monett, Missouri, 103, 113, 114
Monroe County, 137
Morehouse, David, 173, 181
Morrow, John, 50
Mt. Olivet Cemetery, 111
Mount Vernon, Missouri, 70, 163
Mountain Grove, Missouri, 141
Movie star ghosts, 22, 23, 24, 135, 140
Murder Rocks, 155, 156

Nathan Boone Homestead, 83
Nevada, Missouri, 143
Newland, John, 46
Nîmes, France, 11
Nixa, Missouri, 148
Noel, Missouri, 135, 136
North Lawn Cemetery, 140
Northview Community Center, 18

O'Reilly General Army Hospital, O'Reilly Hospital, 56
Oaklawn Cemetery, 141
Old Baptist Cemetery, 111
Old City Hospital, 99
Old Footbridge ghost, 31, 97, 98
Old St. Louis Children's Hospital, 98
orbs, 21, 41, 42, 45, 58, 61, 64, 67, 69, 101, 102, 111, 117, 118, 119, 120, 125, 129, 131, 132, 138, 140, 141, 144, 146, 153, 154

Index

Oronogo, 122
Orrick, Missouri, 162
Osage Indian homeland, 102, 103, 104, 144
Outlaw ghosts in Missouri, 123, 122, 117
Ozark, Missouri, 155, 156
Ozark Mountains, 154
Ozarks Afro-American Heritage Museum, 83

Parker, Bonnie, 166
Parkview High School, 25, 34
Paris, Missouri, 137
Peltier, Leonard, 70
Pentecostal, 56
Penn Valley, 131
Pettibone, Jr., Albert, 111
phantom rider on horse, 104
Phelps Grove Park, 49
Pomme de Terre Lake, 148
Pomme de Terre River, 85, 101
Poplar Bluff, Missouri, 142
portal, 108, 148
Possum Trot, Missouri, 148
Power, Tyrone, 135
Presley, Elvis, 20
Price, Sterling, 32
psychic images in a theater, 24, 25
psychometry, 107
Pulaski County, 137, 151
Pythian Castle, 45, 46, 47

Quantrill's Guerillas, Quantrill's Raiders, 161, 162
Queen of the Parks, 17

Ralston Purina Company, 93
Randolph County, 147

remote viewing, 119, 173, 181
residual haunting, 11, 26, 42, 45, 48, 52, 54, 58, 60, 64, 69, 73, 93, 95, 99, 113, 115, 117, 120, 124, 127, 135, 139, 142, 144, 147, 161, 164, 167
RFD 10, 53
Richmond, Missouri, 161
Ritter Springs Park, 68
River Bluff Cave, 68
roan horse ghost, 153
Roaring River State Park, 156
Rockbridge Mill, 141
Rockcliffe Mansion, 111
Roubidoux Cave, 163

Sac River, 83
Salem, Missouri, 139
Salt River, 138
Sands, Julian, 47
Sansone, Charles, 20
Santa Monica Canyon, California, 24
Schifferdecker Home, 125
School of Metaphysics, 154
Scott, Randolph, 22, 23, 24, 135
Sedalia, Missouri, 145
sensitive, 9, 11, 13, 14, 95, 106, 107
Sequiota Park, 69
shadow figures, 13, 26, 31, 32, 42, 45, 49, 53, 58, 67, 68, 70, 72, 73, 75, 77, 82, 83, 86, 87, 90, 92, 93, 96, 98, 99, 100, 102, 104, 105, 111, 115, 116, 117, 119, 120, 125, 126, 129, 130, 131,

Index

132, 134, 136, 137, 139, 140, 141, 142, 143, 144, 145, 146, 148, 151, 152, 153, 154, 156, 163, 167
Shady Inn, 67
Shelbina, Missouri, 138
Shepherd of the Hills, 75, 77
Shoal Creek, 125
Sidney Street Cave, 96
Sigel, Franz, 32
Snidow, Gordon, 137
Sisters of Mercy, 68
Skinker Boulevard, 97
Society for Psychical Research, 93
soldier ghosts, 133, 137, 140, 143, 146, 161
Sons of Confederacy, 138
Sparta, Missouri 163
Spears Graveyard, 141
Spokane, Missouri, 155
Spook Light Road, 160
Springfield Amusement Company, 17
Springfield Land Fill, 50, 51
Springfield, Missouri, 14, 15, 17, 18, 19, 20, 21, 22, 23, 24, 25, 26, 27, 28, 29, 31, 32, 34, 36, 37, 38, 39, 40, 41, 42, 43, 44, 45, 46, 47, 48, 49, 50, 51, 52, 53, 54, 55, 56, 57, 58, 59, 60, 61, 63, 64, 65, 67, 68, 69, 70, 85, 96, 101, 103, 113, 140, 144, 153, 158, 165, 166, 167
Springfield Public Square, 18, 22, 32
Sri Ramakrishna, 3
St. Charles, Missouri, 115

St. Genevieve, Missouri 117
St. Genevieve Memorial Cemetery, 120
St. James, Missouri, 139
St. John's Hospital, 68
St. Louis Art Museum, 97, 98
St. Louis, Missouri, 9, 91, 92, 93, 94, 95, 96, 97, 98, 99, 100, 116, 165, 167
St. Mary's Catholic Cemetery, 136
St. Robert, Missouri 137, 157
Stillwell, Amos, 111
Stockton Lake, 167
Stotts City, Missouri, 163
Strawberry, Judy, 106
Stroud, Robert, 70
Stuart, Gloria, 56
Sultana, 93
Swan Cave Road, 81, 82, 155
Swan Creek Arch Bridge, 103
Swope Park, 131

Table Rock Lake, 171
Talking Rocks Cavern, 75
Thayer, Missouri, 142
The Ghost Files, 177
time travel, 173, 180
touch reader, 106
Trail of Tears, 163
Truman, Harry S., 20, 130, 157, 171, 182
Turner, Kathleen, 60
Tutt, Dave, 36
Twain, Mark, 93, 111, 112, 137, 140, 171

Uhrig, Cave, 96
Umeki, Miyoshi, 140

Index

Union Cemetery, 131, 132, 133
Union Station, 127, 131, 133, 134
University of Central Missouri, 144
U.S. Medical Center for Federal Prisoners, 70

Valle, Marie Louis, 120
Valley Water Mill, 47, 48, 53
Vermont Park, 145
Vernon County, 144

Wabash Depot, 147
Walnut Grove Cemetery, 146
Walnut Street, Kansas City, 127
Warrensburg, Missouri, 144
Waynesville, Missouri, 163
Weaver, Dennis, 122
Webb City, Missouri, 122
Webster County, Missouri, 48, 101, 102,
Wheeler Cemetery, 151
West Plains, Missouri, 141, 167
Westport, Battle of, 127, 167
White River, 48, 79, 103
Whiteman Air Force Base, 145
Wildcat Glades, 126
Wilson Creek National Battlefield, 166
Windyville, Missouri, 154
Witch Ghosts, 157, 158, 159
Woodlock Cemetery, 151
World War II ghost soldiers, 21, 45, 56, 58, 64, 73, 127, 133, 134, 139
Wounded Knee, 76, 77
Wright, Harold Bell, 75

Xenia, Missouri, 171
Xeriscape garden, 49

Younger Brothers, 75, 166, 117, 165
Younger, Cole, 117, 166
Y-Bridge, 105

Zagonyi, Charles, 32
Zagonyi Park, 70